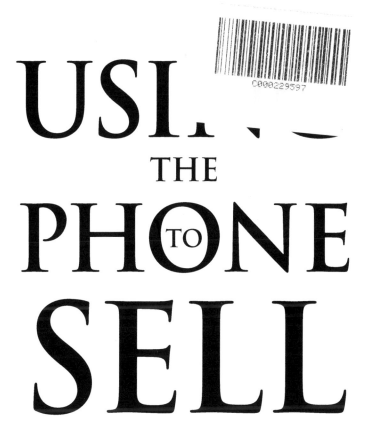

USING
THE
PHONE (TO) SELL

HOW TO SELL MORE TO MORE
PEOPLE MORE OFTEN

ANDREW SEAWARD

Cover image by: D.V.SURESH
Book design by: SWATT Books Ltd

Printed in the United Kingdom
First Printing, 2021

ISBN: 978-1-8383458-0-8 (Paperback)
ISBN: 978-1-8383458-1-5 (eBook)

Andrew Seaward
info@tomarket.co.uk

CONTENTS

CHAPTER 1:
WHY THIS BOOK?

Picture the scene

Imagine it's sometime from the late 1980s onwards, possibly even recently. You're at home, it's early evening, and the phone rings. Your household is a hive of activity as usual. The evening meal is being prepared, the kids are being persuaded to have a bath and the TV is on. The soaps are starting shortly, or possibly it's the game that you want to sit down to watch. The odds that you're going to be at home are at their highest. The phone rings. 'Who's that calling now?'

It's another cold call, trying to persuade you to buy something or other, to agree to a free trial of something or make a charity donation to somebody. The caller is relatively untrained, reciting a script verbatim.

There is no natural tone, warmth, character or personality being projected at all. They don't sound convincing; they're just going through the motions. Possibly anticipating another short call and an abrupt brush-off.

Deviation from their script seems unlikely, as the caller's knowledge begins and ends with the words on the page. You hang up mid-sentence, swear under your breath, and resume your interrupted evening.

Meanwhile, in the call centre, the caller, unsurprised by the abrupt end to yet another call, activates the next number on the list. Only another two hours to go, and at least two of the dozens called so far have agreed to move to the next stage. It's one way to make a living.

We've all experienced this type of business to consumer (B2C) call, or a variation of it. Alternatively, it could be a daytime call at work, this time business to business (B2B), asking you about your phone system, or vehicle fleet, or I.T. supplies. Questions which tell you immediately that the caller knows nothing about your organisation or its present needs.

Intrusive, poorly researched, badly targeted and executed phone calls have made us all wary. Wary of receiving calls if we don't immediately recognise the caller, and therefore, with that experience as a call recipient in our heads, potentially hesitant of deploying the phone as a sales tool, let alone as our primary sales channel.

This is all compounded by the smartphone, which gives us endless ways around actually speaking to someone. 'I'll text him'... 'I'll contact her on Facebook Messenger'... 'I'll DM him on Twitter'... anything to postpone the potential crunch moment of a direct one-to-one conversation. Sending them a message leaves the ball in their court, potentially delaying things for an unspecified time. Meanwhile, who knows? They may be talking to your competitors or engaging with someone who, frankly, makes it easier to buy from.

JUST PICK UP THE PHONE AND MAKE THE CALL!

A phone conversation with your target prospect gets things done. It is quicker than messages backwards and forwards. You initiate a dialogue and decisions get made. You can gently cajole, persuade, and deal with any objections or misunderstandings that may exist. On finding out more about their needs you might sell them a more appropriate product or service. A better solution perhaps.

So, how will this book contribute to the subject of the value of the phone and how best to use it?

The phone as your key B2B sales tool

The focus of this book is selling in a B2B environment rather than a B2C one. B2B is my area of expertise, with decades of experience in a variety of sectors and businesses. Data protection restrictions, made tougher by GDPR in 2018 (more on this later), have particularly affected B2C telephone selling. Cold calling is difficult in B2C markets. B2B, with the widespread scope offered by the level of 'legitimate interest' which a business may have in another business's products or services, mean that this remains a fertile area for professional, targeted, fruitful telephone selling, of benefit to seller AND buyer.

This book aims to restore the reputation of the phone as a business tool. Let's remove that conditioned wariness-from-experience of both recipient and caller. We will provide you with all the tools and techniques you need to conduct well-organised, properly targeted sales calls which achieve results. You'll be given the theory, but also, crucially, the practice.

STORIES FROM THE FRONT

In every chapter, to support specific recommendations, tips and techniques, there are real-life case studies and examples which illustrate and show these points in action. I've called these *Stories from the Front*, as, let's be honest, a sales call or telemarketing campaign can feel like a military campaign at times. Sometimes you feel that you're winning, sometimes you feel you're losing. And sometimes progress can feel like you're moving inches.

Consequently, you need the right bullets and the right armoury to give yourself the best chance of success.

These stories will help you to envisage how best to use a particular technique in your own business environment. Hopefully, some of them will bring a smile too, as you realise that it's not just you who faces these challenges.

As I say more than once in the book, **people buy from people**, and people are of course at times unpredictable in their attitudes and reactions to any given sales situation. These stories show how real people react to real situations. Some of them are light-hearted, as seeing the comedy in a situation is often the best way through it!

Making outbound calls? Read on!

This book is for anyone who needs to make outbound sales calls. Within that broad definition, there are various roles:

- **An employee making sales calls.** You might be selling products or services to customers on the phone. Or maybe you set appointments for field-based colleagues on the phone. Possibly your job is to generate leads for somebody else or for yourself.

- **Part of a field-based sales team.** Here, you need to make your own sales appointments. Maybe you spend a set number of days in the office. For example, two days out on the road going to see customers, two days in the office setting appointments for future weeks, and one day doing administration.

- **Somebody who manages a team making outbound phone calls.** If you are a supervisor, team leader or manager, you need to ensure that the team is organised, focused, motivated and able to achieve results.

- **A self-employed freelance consultant.** Someone who relies on the phone to generate new business. There are proposals to follow up, lapsed clients to reconnect with and new prospects to communicate with.

- **A business leader or entrepreneur.** You may have an interest in knowing how the telephone can be used more effectively to generate new business.

Prospecting pre-the telephone

The telephone as a tool for prospecting has had a chequered past. Back in the '60s and '70s, field-based salespeople were encouraged to simply knock on doors. Years ago, I used to work for a forklift truck company. At the time when I joined, in the mid-80s, door-knocking was still the principal way for the field salespeople to generate new prospects. They would be instructed to take one of the company's small pallet trucks on the back of a trailer, expected to park it up in the middle of the industrial estate, walk around and start banging on some doors. In fact, the company insisted on this type of activity. If a salesman (and they were largely men at that point) was reluctant to carry out this activity, the territory sales manager would go out with them. Sometimes, the whole sales team of six people and their manager would travel around industrial estates together. The idea was that they would all be supporting each other, and it was intended to be motivational for the team. A bit of male bonding if you like. And boy, was this approach successful?! The company I worked for was a highly effective sales organisation. I'm not saying that it was simply because they went out door-knocking, but they were a progressive company working with a field salesforce of around 50 people. They figured out what worked.

Clearly, much has changed since then. By the mid-80s the telephone had become a potential new tool to use to contact more people in less time, and at a lower cost. Part of the problem with having a large field-based salesforce is that it is incredibly expensive. In this B2B organisation, each of the sales team was a professional, paid good money and motivated with good bonuses. To have them tramping round industrial states knocking on doors and asking,

"Excuse me, do you want to buy a forklift truck?" was an ineffective use of their time.

I joined the company in a marketing capacity, and my boss Tony was a bit of a visionary. An excellent problem solver. He was interested in exploring the idea of using telemarketing to develop prospecting within the company in a more cost-effective way.

Early phone prospecting

In the 1980s, telephone teams and contact centres started to spring up around the UK. Employing a team of dedicated telemarketers, as well as a supervisor, manager, and a backup admin team, was likely to be more cost effective than having a highly paid team out on the road doing the same job.

The theory was that each telemarketer could speak to around 25 decision makers every day, from the comfort of the office. They would be trained how to do this properly. Consequently, they could do this day-in, day-out for 48 weeks in a year. For the salesman operating out in the field, prospecting was always a bit of a compromise. They also had to visit current customers. This might be to talk about new opportunities, or it might be to calm things down if something had gone wrong. They also had to write sales proposals and attend sales meetings. So, to have a dedicated telephone-based team was a much purer prospecting model.

Telephone calls, when conducted professionally in B2B environments, became an effective way of increasing a company's prospect pot. However, as we all know, use of the telephone for this purpose became corrupted over time. Just as professional companies recognised the power of the telephone, so did slightly less scrupulous B2C companies as well.

Many companies would employ people, often on commission only, pass them the *Yellow Pages* or some other form of telephone directory and tell them to, *"Phone some people in there."* The idea was of course that if the person wasn't successful in the role, they wouldn't earn much or anything at all. Or the employer could simply fire them. In most of these instances the new recruits would generally be young. This would perhaps be their first job. What a welcome to the world of work!

Tarnishing the phone's reputation

Customers' experience of this type of phoning clearly damaged the reputation of outbound telemarketing. The person making the call was untrained and consequently had a script that they weren't allowed to deviate from. The reason they weren't allowed to deviate from the script, of course, was that they had no conversational abilities or sales skills over and above what the sales manager or company owner had decided they needed. This is how the telephone as a prospecting tool acquired its terrible image. To a large degree it was irreparably damaged. It's never really recovered, especially in B2C industries. Even the phrase 'cold calling' makes people shudder. It's bad enough if you've got to take these types of calls. But imagine the horror if you actually need to make some for your own business. This level of fear frequently migrates over into B2B environments. Understandably, field sales or even some telesales or telemarketing people dread making cold calls. This is because they know how they feel when they receive them at home.

B2B telephone selling works

There is a world of difference between those new recruits making calls to you at home trying to sell stuff you don't need, compared with a professionally trained person in a B2B environment.

In business to business, hopefully the person making the calls is more highly paid and so they are a resource that you cannot afford to waste. Training is important. You might expect me to say that. But so are other things such as targeting. It's well worth spending time carefully targeting the companies that will be contacted. For me, this makes more difference to the effectiveness of any telephoning campaign than even the skills of the person making the call.

This brings me on to those of us who do, or should, make some prospecting calls for their own business: self-employed or freelance consultants.

Freelance consultants

I'm aware there are a growing number of self-employed freelance people who work in some form of business consultancy. So, you have a product (well it's a service really) which is your intellect. You have no physical product to show anybody or display on your website. But you have a business, and a need to earn money. Clearly, you need to sell your services to potential prospects but how do you do this? You have nothing to show, other than perhaps your smiley face. You also want to tell people that you know an impressive amount about your subject and are really good! The key challenge though for anybody in consultancy is how do you communicate that on the telephone? We will give you some answers!

The power of the phone

The telephone is an immensely powerful tool to use in conducting business. We use it to talk to current customers. We use it to set up meetings, and we use it socially. Theoretically then, there is no reason why we shouldn't use it to generate new prospects. After all, what's the worst that can happen? They'll say 'No.' They might not be interested. But surely there are bigger challenges in your day. The good news is that somebody might actually want to buy something from you!

The telephone allows you to have a personalised one to one conversation with another human being, hopefully without any additional distractions. You can talk about them and their business. You will find out about their thoughts and feelings. This of course allows you to tailor what you say back to them. These are all powerful reasons why the telephone is a great medium to use. You can't achieve this level of dialogue with any form of 'push' marketing: letters, adverts, or general social media.

Furthermore, you can do this from the comfort of your office or even your home if you're lucky. The costs are low. If you're employed, but working from home, presumably you can claim these against expenses. You won't be wearing out your shoe leather, and you won't even need to start up your car or use public transport. It all has so much going for it.

It's much more popular currently to use social media for your marketing. And I'm not saying that you shouldn't use social media. I'm a big believer that it has a place in the marketing mix. It's here to stay, and therefore you should learn how to make the best use of it. It's not for every type of business, but it's important for most.

The great attraction of social media is that it is free. This is fantastic, as it allows everyone to access it in the same way. It doesn't matter whether your business is just you working from home, or you're a multinational company, you have equal access to the internet. However, its strength has also become its weakness. The very fact that it's free, means that everyone is doing it. There is no reason not to, apart from the fact that it takes some time, often a considerable amount of time.

The fact that everyone is doing it, therefore means that there is a lot of noise out there. How on earth do you get your voice heard above all the clamour? This book does not set out to answer that question.

If you view the marketing mix as a sort of scale, then the telephone sits somewhere in the middle. It's not as good in terms of quality as physically sitting in front of a customer, sharing a coffee at their desk. But it is much better quality than any mass form of marketing you do, such as advertising or social media. It's not free, but then it doesn't cost anything like as much as going to see somebody.

And the downside

While in this book I am championing the phone and showing you ways in which to maximise its potential, I am not blind to its pitfalls and weaknesses. OK, so it's not such a good quality conversation as when you're sat with somebody. I've also observed over the last 20 years that it's getting considerably more difficult to get through to the person that you want to speak to: the decision-maker. People are often busy, and of course we need to acknowledge that frequently they simply don't want to take your call! This is when you are told by the receptionist that they're in a meeting. I've always been a bit of a geeky analyst, and so I have always monitored all my outbound call activity. I record how many dials I make, the number of hours I'm phoning, as well as the number of decision makers I get through to. This is known as the DMP rate (decision-maker presentations). More on this later.

The bad news is that this rate has decreased significantly over the last 20 years. I now get through to around half the decision makers per hour than I used to. This is discouraging of course, but it brings you back to the key question, 'What is the most effective use of your marketing time?' And of course, if you're employed to make outbound calls, all you can do is try your best to come up with creative ways of trying to get through to people.

The phone is just part of the marketing mix

Any form of marketing needs to be part of a blend of activities. So hopefully you and your company will send mailshots to people. You'll also be sending regular e-flyers, and you'll be busy on social media. Then of course there's advertising, articles in trade magazines and exhibitions. Let's not forget PR too.

If you're running your own business, or you are a freelance operator, then my suggestion as a marketeer is that you should again consider all forms of marketing. The correct marketing mix for you will depend on your industry sector. If you're a solo business, it will probably also depend on your personality to a large degree.

If you don't enjoy writing, then regular blogging probably isn't for you. If you're great technically, but uncomfortable in the company of strangers then I wouldn't advocate doing networking. If it fills you with dread, then what's the point? However, as I've already stated, people buy from people, and business networking provides you with an ideal environment in which to get directly in front of people and start the meet > like > know > trust process that is an essential part of selling. However, I would suggest that trying a bit of all these types of things is probably worth the effort. You may be surprised to discover what works best for you.

Product v. service definitions

This book is littered with references to products and services. Here are my definitions of these two terms. It should also be noted that, for the purposes of this book, nearly all the selling lessons I talk about work equally well with products and services.

For me, a product is something tangible. Something you can touch. Accountants, in a rare touch of light humour when carrying out audits, describe stock as something you can kick!

A service therefore is something people pay for, but which isn't physical. I'm sure you've worked this out already. So, if you're working in the construction industry selling consumables then these are all products. However, if you sell insurance, or any form of business consultancy, then these are of course services.

Develop your strategy

The telephone is a powerful medium for maintaining contact with current customers. It's also great for generating new leads and sales opportunities. You will need to develop different strategies for both these types of customers. With your current customers, phone calls are an easy way of staying close to them. You want to talk to them regularly, because you want to build the relationship and rapport with them. If you ignore them, or don't talk to them frequently enough, you are opening up that account to attack from your competition. And it is important to recognise, just as with *Stories from the Front*, that this type of military language is entirely appropriate in this situation. We all operate in a competitive environment. Ultimately your customer will only remain loyal while they believe that you are their best option. You want to talk to them and find out their thoughts and feelings. You want to introduce them to new products, and you will also be looking for additional sales opportunities. There may well be some products you supply that they are not currently buying from you. Or you can look for opportunities to upgrade them onto more expensive, and better-quality products. There are frequently sales opportunities within your current customer base. It's important that you keep beavering away.

New leads and lapsed customers

Your new leads strategy may in part involve some cold calling. Approaching some companies that you know should use your types of products, but who you've not traded with before. Be aware of the opportunities within lapsed accounts too. It's difficult to define what the definition of lapsed is. If your industry generally has customers who are on five-year contracts, then clearly a current customer might not have bought anything from you for four and a half years. But they are still current, they are not lapsed. In other industries where perhaps there is some seasonality in purchasing, probably anyone who hasn't bought from you within a year might be considered to be lapsed. Either way, I consider lapsed customers to be a fantastic source of future business. The very fact that they bought from you in the past, means that you have a reason for engaging in dialogue with them. It might be of course that their processes have changed, and they may no longer have a use for the type of products you sell. Fair enough. At least you know. With every lapsed customer, ideally you want to have had a conversation with them so that you know why they are no longer buying from you. Some of these you may never get back, but there will still be plenty of opportunity elsewhere.

Cold calling

In addition to the calls you make to your regular customers, plus some contact with lapsed customers, it's important that you mix in some cold calls. If you're an employee, this may already be set for you. But if you are self-employed or trying to generate your own business over the phone, then this is something you should choose to do. Whilst I understand that cold calls represent the scary end of outbound calling, nevertheless mixing in a few of these on a regular basis is a vital part of the marketing mix. To grow any business, it's important to keep pushing and winning new customers. The maths of this are easy to understand. If you have 100 customers after year one, and you put all your efforts into working with these, inevitably some will drift away. However good you, your company and your products are. You might find by the end of year one you have 87 customers. Maintaining the same strategy may result in just 75 customers by the end of year 2. You get the picture. Ultimately, the business will simply heal over and die. One way or another then, we need to find ways of generating new customers.

The importance of targeting

The key to good and effective cold calling is targeting. I cannot make this point strongly enough. Every hour spent by you or your marketing colleagues on defining your target market is invaluable. Time spent working out who you should be talking to - will easily be repaid once you start working on the phone. **You need a reason to talk to people.** One of many things most of us don't like about receiving cold calls at home, is that they are completely indiscriminate. Going back to that early evening call, you know instantly that the person calling just sees you as the next number on their list. There is almost never any pre-call planning conducted. Usually in B2C calls they know nothing about you. Frequently they won't even know your name. Consequently, the whole process from their perspective is completely impersonal. That's part of the reason that I've generally stayed away from working within B2C markets. I much prefer B2B. You are a professional person, attempting to make a call to another professional person. If you can see your call structure in that light, hopefully it may give you more confidence to make outbound calls.

Build your list

Spend some desk time working out which organisations could potentially use your products or services. If you're starting outbound telephoning or telemarketing from scratch, then you will need to spend a few hours building your target list. However, for most of you, you'll be working within a business that already has an established customer base. In this case it's a little easier, as you are simply trying to top up your marketing database or contact list.

Open your mind to the possibilities around you. You might read an article about a company in your area. You might not have spoken to them before, but you know because of the industry sector they are in, that they could use what you sell. Just driving about or commuting on the bus or train will frequently give you many ideas. You may see a van or a truck. You might be sat at the traffic lights and notice a commercial building nearby. If you're a field-based salesperson, chances are you'll frequently be making trips onto business parks or industrial estates. Have a look at what's around as you approach your destination. These are all effective ways of finding new names. And who knows? One of these might just be your next big customer. You have nothing to lose.

The longer you have been working in the business, the more you will instinctively have an idea about the types of companies that may have a use for your products. Identifying the type of industry sector that the target company might be in is perhaps one of the more obvious elements of targeting. Why not consider contacting the competitors of some of your customers? In some situations, you may need to be careful with this, as you could potentially jeopardise a major account. Generally, though, this is unlikely to be a major problem. Especially if you're selling lower ticket price consumable items.

Also consider the size of the company. How big do they need to be, for them to be relevant for your organisation? You can measure this in terms of either turnover or number of employees. If it's important to know their precise size before you contact them, there are many places online where you can find this information. These services are usually based on financial accounts. You or your company may need to pay for a subscription to obtain detailed accounts. You can also buy lists of companies to set criteria from commercial list brokers.

There are many brokers still offering these services, even post-GDPR. If you intend buying in lists, ensure you do your homework thoroughly first. Check that this is a reputable and fully compliant seller. If you contact potential customers in breach of GDPR rules, the consequences could be significant. You need to give careful thought to the categories you want to select. Many will include all sorts of businesses you're not able to sell to. You probably want to leave out multi-site organisations too. If you sell workwear and consumables to the trade, you probably don't want every branch of Travis Perkins and Homebase, do you?

I recommend that you obtain a sample of any list you intend buying, ahead of making a commitment to buy it. That way you can check your assumptions. Clearly, any bought-in list represents the coldest types of calls there are. Consequently, there are a host of reasons why you should avoid buying in cold lists.

Start building relationships

The scariest element of cold calling is making that first call and making that initial presentation to a decision maker. However, because I do nearly all my business generation using the telephone, I find it helpful to reassure myself that every new customer starts with that cold call. The key is to know what to say and how to structure your call. If you feel comfortable with that, and about why you are making the call, you should have little to fear.

Track down a name

The first thing you need to do is to navigate your way past the gatekeeper. Usually this is the receptionist. We'll cover this in more detail in Chapter 9. So, let's consider what happens on one of those one-in-four calls where you do get through to the person you want to speak to. Incidentally, if you can find out the name of the person you need to speak to in advance it will make the job easier. It sounds less like a cold call to a receptionist if you ask for somebody by name. *"Could I speak to Sarah Pearson please?"* will probably make you feel more confident than simply asking for 'the person who deals with your stationery.' There are many ways that you can try and find the name of the right contact in advance. The most obvious one, accessible to most people, is LinkedIn.

Sometimes you may not be able to find the name of the exact person that you want to speak to at your target company. In this situation, simply look for somebody with a job title which is the best of what is available. I might look for the head of learning and development in a target company. I might not be able to find them, but perhaps I can find an HR business partner. They are probably a good person to establish contact with. They are close enough to almost certainly know who I would need to speak to. Once you get hold of them, they will gladly tell you who you need to speak to. That's because it's not them, and they want to get you off their hands!

If you're targeting the sales manager, or the sales director, then perhaps the office manager would be a useful contact. Or maybe you find an account manager on LinkedIn. If they are in a field-based role, they will inevitably know who the most senior sales contact is in their organisation. It is almost certainly their boss or their boss's boss.

The MD isn't necessarily the contact you want

In the old days of telemarketing, by which I mean the 1980s, many telemarketers would be told that they needed to focus on making contact with the managing director. Generally, I would advise against this. The theory is of course that they are ultimately the person who must sign off any work or purchasing decisions. Furthermore, if they refer you to somebody else, you are in a strong position of being able to say, *"Ok, Jane, your managing director suggested I speak to you."* It's great in theory, but it seldom works in practice. The managing director, or CEO, will inevitably be the person who is most protected against taking unsolicited calls. Clearly, if they spent all their day taking sales calls, they wouldn't be able to get on with the more important job of running their company. Consequently, you are extremely unlikely to get through. However, this does depend to some degree on the size of the business you are targeting. The larger the company you are contacting, the less likely you are to get through. If you are trying to contact the CEO of a Footsie 100 company, they will inevitably be extremely well guarded. Also, people in those types of roles will inevitably spend 8 to 10 hours a day in meetings or on conference calls.

Conversely, if you're trying to contact the managing director or owner of a small company, they will probably be far more accessible. A client I work with has a network of five or six retail outlets serving tradesmen across the Midlands. It's run by a very hands-on managing director. He makes most of the decisions and is quite easy to get hold of. The most common reason I can't contact him on the telephone is because he's out visiting customers. But other than that, he is generally easy to get hold of.

Establish a relationship

It's important to consider the type of organisation and the person you are trying to get hold of. If you're trying to get hold of somebody at a senior level in a target company, you may well be able to find out much of what you need by talking to other people.

So, be patient and play the long game. Inevitably with any new company you are trying to contact, ultimately your aim is to sell them something. That's completely understandable. You might on some occasions get through to the decision maker and find that they thank you for calling. You may end the call with a sale. If you can achieve this, then you've done extremely well, and you've probably been lucky. This won't happen often. Therefore, I suggest that the way of viewing your efforts on cold calls is to simply start building a relationship. I would go so far as to say try not to sell. Especially if you are in a market sector where you are selling high-priced items or consultative types of services. The same goes for industry sectors where a new potential client would be taking a considerable risk in giving you all their business, such as transport and logistics.

When making cold calls or trying to establish a relationship with somebody you've not worked with before, it's important to see this as a long process. A let's-get-to-know-each-other-a-bit type of thing. Be prepared to use your range of communication skills to start building rapport. Once you've got their attention on the phone, ask them some questions. These will generally be about their business and potentially their personal role in the organisation. Make sure that you listen to them and take notes. **It's more important to listen than it is to talk, especially in these early stages.**

Once you have found out a little bit of information about them, then that gives you the chance to tailor what you say back to them. Relate your products or services directly to what the decision maker has just said to you. That way it proves that you are listening, and the conversation will likely be more engaging for them. The more relevant it is to them, the more interested they are likely to be. By all means tell them things about your company or business but keep it fairly brief. Make it related to what you do for customers rather than what you are. An example might be that you could say to them:

> *".... ok that's interesting that you supply to the healthcare industry. We have a specific range of products in our healthcare division that is specifically intended for companies such as yours."*

This is far better than you saying something like:

> *"We're a company that's been in business for 127 years, now run by the 5th generation of the family. We sell 10,000 products and have 1,500 customers in the UK alone."*

You may be impressed by your company's heritage, but it's unlikely that the customer will, because it doesn't show them any benefit.

Generally speaking, you'll probably want to avoid talking about prices in the early part of the conversation. Unless they ask. In which case you don't want to avoid their direct question. But generally, try not to get involved in too much granular detail at this stage. Keep your conversation light. It's perhaps a bit like dating. You don't necessarily want to ask this total stranger out on a date as your first question. Spend a bit of time getting to know the decision maker and their business.

Your primary objective on this first call may be to simply make them aware there is a company out there who specialises in providing products or services for their application. You might aim to give them a take-away fact about you or your company. That's all fine. If they are an engineering company, you might want to drop into the conversation that you supply Rolls Royce aero engines with some of your products. If you're selling a consultancy type of service, again you may want to talk about a particular project that you worked on recently which is similar to their application. Or again you may name-drop a well-known client. At this point you simply want to reassure them that you could help.

Your questioning should be business related. Find out where they are in the buying cycle. If you sell large ticket capital equipment items, such as a large industrial printer or a forklift truck, you will almost certainly want to know when they last purchased, and when they expect to be in the market again. Don't be side-tracked by the glamour of the large pieces of kit either. There are always opportunities to remind new prospects that you supply a full range of consumables as well. The very fact that a potential customer uses a large piece of capital equipment inevitably means they use certain consumables as well.

Try to find out who they buy from, and something about what they buy and their volumes. To a great degree, your success here in asking what some might see as impertinent questions will be based on how effective you've been in building rapport with them. Clearly, if they're feeling comfortable with you, and they are fairly open, they will probably give you this information willingly. Conversely, if you come across as being too 'salesy' and they're waiting for the inevitable sales pitch, chances are they'll be far more guarded.

STORIES FROM THE FRONT

I remember years ago I undertook some telephone skills training with a UK based reprographics company down in the South West. They supplied large format printing machines to commercial printers. But of course, they also sold the consumables, such as the inks to go with them. Somebody using a printer must by definition be buying ink to put in it. One of the things I remember their managing director Roger saying to me was that he believed the telephone sales team often missed out on these smaller opportunities. On the telephone they would focus on the potential of the large format printers but wouldn't get involved in conversations about the inks. And of course, as is the case with many companies, the margin is often far greater on the consumables than it is with the original machine. It's the same with your printer at home of course. Chances are, like me you'll be amazed at how cheap the printer is, but then equally amazed at how expensive the ink cartridges are.

It used to be the same in the forklift truck industry. Companies would typically compete and reduce prices just to get their forklift truck into a client company. Often a deal would be won, at wafer thin margins. It was the job of the service division to then make up the profit over the life of the truck. I think this is a typical business model.

It's like the Midlands' retailer I know with shops supplying tradesmen. The boss, Gary, wants his sales staff to always ask about boxes of screws at the till. Relatively low cost, certainly low emotional involvement, but a good profitable line for the company.

Establish follow-up contact

As I've already mentioned, just establishing contact with a prospective client for the first time may be a good objective. If you're able to follow this up with any next action, then so much the better. As a result of the things that you've spoken about during the call, you might offer to send them something by email. Or you might send them a PDF type document. You may feel that you got on well enough to make a connection through LinkedIn. *At the very least you want to finish the call by agreeing when you will contact them next.* Even if they are happy with their current supplier and give you the clear intention that there is no opportunity for you for the foreseeable future, still look to build some continuity into the relationship. You might finish the call by saying something like, *"Ok, well it sounds like you're fairly well sorted for the time being, but I'd like to keep in touch. I'll give you a call in six months' time if that's alright."* **Very, very** rarely will somebody decline this. And in fact, if they do, it's best that you know now.

Prepare for the call

In summary, provided you've done your research in advance, and know why this company and why this human being could potentially use your products or services, you're off to a good start. Be totally clear in your own mind why you're calling. If you're not sure, spend a bit of desk time thinking about it before you pick up the phone. It's highly likely that you will be asked this very question by any decision maker you get through to. So, it pays to be prepared.

Practice makes perfect

The only other piece of advice I'd offer at this stage about making outbound prospecting calls is that, like any skill, it takes practice. There are very few things in life that we are good at the first time we try them. Furthermore, if you can be good at something the first time you do it, it isn't really a skill. Ultimately what gives us satisfaction in life is developing a new skill. *So, being successful at outbound telephoning will require practice, practice, practice.* If your phone calls are part of a mixed role then always try to allocate blocks of at least an hour at a time to phoning. You need to get into the groove. It's difficult to get any momentum going if you're only making one or two calls at a time before going off to do something else. And remember that over time 100 hours spent on the phone is far more useful to you than 10 hours. And inevitably 1,000 hours is a lot better still.

There's no easy way around this. You need to dive in and start swimming. Just to keep that metaphor going a little longer, hopefully what's contained in this book will give you some tips not just to help you stay afloat, but to swim to your destination.

In the following chapters are some tips and techniques, plus some ways to make effective phone calls, all based on proven experience. I realise that it's about confidence too, especially if telemarketing isn't your main job role. But if some of what you read in the subsequent chapters helps you feel more confident about doing this work, then that is my job done.

GDPR & the legal framework

The General Data Protection Regulation rules (GDPR) were introduced as a piece of EU legislation in May 2018. There are fundamentally two parts to these laws, which saw a tightening of data protection laws that were already in existence.

GDPR essentially covers two elements of customer protection. The primary one is around restricting contact between companies and prospective customers. Unless the customer has specifically given permission to be contacted by a company, then it is illegal for a seller to make contact. This even applies to regular customers.

Consequently, companies generally use a double opt-in for customers to agree to receive communication. In practice, the way this works is that you sign up on the website to receive their regular newsletter. This is then followed by an automated email from the company saying, *"Are you sure you want to receive communication from us?"*

All this opt-in agreement communication can be recorded, stored, and therefore audited at a later date. This enables companies to ensure that they are fully compliant.

I did sense that within a few months of the new laws coming into effect, many companies were either bending the rules or flagrantly disregarding them. A huge loophole appears to be that companies can make contact if they can show 'legitimate interest' is in evidence. However, this is such a vague phrase, open to all sorts of different interpretations, that it has left the door open to unscrupulous practitioners to effectively ignore any of the designed (and welcome) restraints of GDPR. As a result, within six to nine months I was receiving as many unsolicited sales emails as I had previously. Maybe you have had a similar experience.

So, where does all this leave us? I would always recommend that, regardless of the laws in place, you should always work to ensure that your targeting is accurate. Even if it isn't illegal, you don't do your company's reputation any good if you're contacting potential buyers indiscriminately. If they have no potential use for your products or services, then they will be likely to view negatively any approach you make.

The second element behind the GDPR rules relates to protecting customer data. You must ensure that it is well protected and encrypted so that it cannot easily be accessed by external third parties such as computer hackers. We've all read those embarrassing stories in the news of civil servants or other business people leaving on the train laptops containing tens of thousands of customer records, including addresses and full bank details. Each organisation which stores customer data now needs to nominate a data controller. That person is legally responsible for ensuring full compliance with these new laws. Fines for abuse of GDPR have now been set as high as 4% of annual global turnover, up to a maximum of €20M, so this is a law which potentially has sharp teeth. Aside from the financial penalties, the longer-lasting damage could be to the organisation's reputation as one to be trusted with anyone's data, or as a business you would feel comfortable working for.

GDPR was an EU initiative but post-Brexit it, or a similar version of it, will still be in place. The Information Commissioner's Office (ICO), which oversees data issues in the UK, issued this guidance at the end of 2020:

> *The government has said that it intends to incorporate the GDPR into UK data protection law from the end of the transition period – so in practice there will be little change to the core data protection principles, rights and obligations found in the GDPR.*

The EU version of the GDPR may also still apply directly to you if you operate in Europe, offer goods or services to individuals in Europe, or monitor the behaviour of individuals in Europe.

The GDPR will still apply to any organisations in Europe who send you data, so you may need to help them decide how to transfer personal data to the UK in line with the GDPR.

Whenever you read this book, the situation may have changed, but whatever the regulatory framework, you need to take seriously your approach to handling client and prospect data.

CHAPTER 2:
WHAT IS SELLING?

This book is intended to relate directly to people who make outbound telephone calls in pursuit of some form of sale. Of course, there are many different versions of the outcome of those calls. You may sell products directly. Or you may set appointments for one of your colleagues to go and visit the customer. The third possibility is that you're setting appointments for yourself, to go out and meet somebody. In any of these situations you are making outbound calls with a view to achieving something which is all part of the sales process.

Selling in the UK seems to have a bad image. It appears, for any of us involved in any part of the sales process, that we are inherently not to be trusted, that we're slimy and generally people not capable of doing a job with a more intellectual bias. That's highly unfortunate, because it doesn't have this image in many other countries. The United States is one such example, where professional salespeople are respected and looked up to.

This attitude in the UK is a great shame because, like anything else, selling is a skill. There are people who are good at it and there are people who are not so good at it. However, a good professional salesperson will be someone who helps you to introduce a new product or service into your life, where you feel happy with your overall experience. You will inevitably have warmed to them as a person, and you will feel they're interested in you, whilst also keeping an eye on the interests of their company or employer.

Selling as a concept

For me, selling is a broad concept. We will often come across the idea that salespeople are born, not made. People will use phrases like, *"He had the gift of the gab"*, meaning presumably they had lots to say and were persuasive, perhaps! Then you get other comments such as *"He could sell ice to the Eskimos" "She could sell sand to the Arabs."* And some of the less savoury ones, such as *"They would even sell their grandmother if they had to."*

These are all references to communication skills. It's certainly true that some people are naturally more communicative than others. Somebody perhaps that works in a more technical role will frequently not be the life and soul of a party or a 'I'm here – look at me' kind of personality. Nevertheless, I believe that people can be trained to sell. For me, it's not about the fact that somebody either has the ability or they don't.

Selling is described as both an art and a science. Those who subscribe to the former view say a salesman is *"born a salesman"*, with the implication that if you don't have the necessary skills in-born, then you're never likely to be successful in sales.

However, seeing selling as a science opens up the idea that skills can be taught and improved upon. By considering it as a process, we can all be more effective in how we undertake it.

What is selling?

There are many definitions for what sales is. This simple one from the Oxford Dictionary is that selling is to *'give or hand over (something) in exchange for money.'*

Of course, it is this, but even in the list of dictionary definitions it also talks about selling ideas. At its heart, selling is something quite simple:

Selling is the art of persuasion

Consequently, selling is something that everybody does at some point every day. We make sales pitches frequently without even consciously thinking about it, but we're selling, nonetheless. So, the idea that somebody is born to be a natural seller is overly simplistic.

We all need to develop sales skills – just to get on in life. We sell ideas. We sell ourselves; we sell solutions, and we sell products and services. Furthermore, just by going to work we are trading. You swap your time for money. You build up money for your house, for holidays, for your hobbies etc.

Life is competitive. You sold yourself to your partner (current and previous!). Dating is partly about getting to know each other. Then when you're keen, you up the selling! You are trying to get them to see that you are the best one for them. Ultimately, by making a long-term commitment such as marriage, you are persuading them that you are the correct life partner! Big powerful stuff isn't it? You sell yourself when you are applying for a job. Whether you're filling in the application form, or attending an interview, you're selling. What you are selling of course is you! Undoubtedly, you're selling hard in this instance. For the job you are in now, you sold successfully. For that dream job you applied for, that you didn't get, someone else sold themselves more effectively.

It's competitive. Someone wins, someone loses. It can be a cruel world, but this is the way the world works.

7 characteristics of successful salespeople

As we have said, selling can be considered as both art and science. But it's more than this. It's all very well having creative flair in the way you communicate with customers and prospects. And it's great if you know the process from start to finish, and inside out. But if you don't fundamentally *believe* in it, and communicate that to your customers, then it will all fall a bit flat. If you don't believe in it, then why should they? **So, you must have passion.** If you don't believe in it, the benefit of what you are offering, and if it doesn't enthuse you, it's time to go off and do something else.

I've worked alongside many successful salespeople over the years, and I've observed some of the personal characteristics they all seem to have in common. I should point out that these are purely anecdotal characteristics that I have noticed about them. This is not a scientific list, as there are so many nuances to effective selling.

Simply being in the presence of other people, watching them and listening to them in their sales roles, has given me huge cues and tips which I use every day now.

Personality types are numerous, and a group of salespeople is no different to any other subset of the population. Nevertheless, I have identified 7 key characteristics in the professional salespeople I've worked with over the years.

1. Creativity of thought
2. Methodical approach to selling activity
3. Belief in what they're doing
4. Mental toughness and resilience
5. Ambition
6. Good interpersonal skills
7. Good communication skills

1. Creativity of thought

We need to be creative when selling. And no, I don't mean making things up or lying! Not creative in the way that 'creative accounting' is meant!

You will often be part of a sales process where you feel that you are selling square pegs to someone who has round holes. It is then important to think about the customer's situation and the product or service's application from various different angles.

Let's develop the square pegs and round holes analogy a bit further, as far-fetched as it sounds. Maybe you could get your colleagues to round off those square pegs so that they fit the customer's round holes. Maybe that's the way the market is going anyway. Your company needs to adapt fast. It's all about round holes these days. Square holes are so yesterday. Like IBM computers, the local fishmongers, greengrocers, and retail shopping. Adapt or die. You get the picture. Another approach might be to find out why the customer believes that round holes are important. Maybe you sell square pegs because square holes are now much more efficient than the old round ones. You may be showing the customer a better, more efficient, cost-effective way of doing things. You're helping them survive.

Maybe the customer wants 12 of an item but you only have 7 in stock. Theoretically, you're unable to supply them what they want. But with some creative thinking, you may be able to come up with a solution to suit both of you. Even if it's not a perfect solution, it's important to try and secure the customer where you can. Because, if your answer is *"No, I can't help you"*, they will start talking to one of your competitors. At that point everything they spend with you is up for grabs. It then depends on the quality of that other salesperson.

Selling products - what options do you have?

Maybe they are looking to order 12 because that is the number they always buy. Perhaps they don't need all of them at this time. Your questioning will help you find this out. Or perhaps they buy them in twelves because your company gives them a better bulk discount rate. Once you know that, you have options, you have wriggle room. There are things you can do. Maybe you could sell them 7 now, and then put the other 5 units on call-off order, perhaps at the same price as you would normally sell them 12. After all, that's fair isn't it? It is not the customer's fault that you do not have 12 in stock at present. Therefore, it's reasonable that you try to make sure that they are not paying more to take these 12 units from you. There are many ways of cutting this, but the key is to think creatively. There are not always obvious ways out, but with a bit of thought, you can often come up with great solutions to suit both parties. Sometimes you'll even amaze yourself!

Selling services

For those of you in consultancy-type businesses, what you sell is what is in your head. That is your product, and consequently you have a limited supply. There are only so many hours in a day that you can work, and swap time for money. You will often uncover opportunities that don't quite fit what you do. On occasions, the client may be asking for something which you know isn't really in your skill set. It may be similar to what you specialise in, and so therefore to the client it seems a reasonable question to ask. At other times, you may be asked to carry out work, and after checking your diary, you know you do not have the time to allocate to this at the moment. If you are self-employed, you have complete control over how you deal with these situations.

A creative solution would be to look for other consultants that you can work collaboratively with. It is worth building up these other relationships, as you don't know when you may need them. Clearly, you want to build up relationships with people that you can trust, especially if you are offering them work with your clients. You may even set the work up so that they are working under your business's name. It is vital to feel that you can trust them, and that they will represent your business in the same way that you would. After all, you've spent time developing your businesses image and goodwill, haven't you?

The power of collaboration

These collaborative relationships are well worth developing. It means that you can say *"yes"* to more things. If a client comes to you with a specific piece of work, having collaborative relationships already built up means that you can say *"yes"* rather than *"not now"*. Again, the danger with *"not now"* is that if you say that to them on this occasion, they may well end up looking for and engaging with other consultants for other future pieces of work. Especially if they decide they like them and get on well with them. In any form of self-employed work, you are selling them you. And you don't want them to go off and develop a new best friend elsewhere, do you?

There are many other benefits to collaborations too. You will obviously give thought to how you will remunerate your chosen business partner. There are two ways I have done this in the past. The first is to simply pass them the work. You request some form of commission. A finder's fee. Doing it this way means that you don't get involved in the work at all. Your business partner carries out the work, organises all the invoicing, and then must wait for payment. They work under their own business name. This means that you get a bit of commission, for probably not doing a lot. If this arrangement involves a regular customer of yours, you may want to have a phone conversation or perhaps meet them to explain why you're offering this piece of work to your trusted business partner. But by and large this is a relatively hands-off approach.

An alternative way of managing the relationship is to commission this business partner to work under your banner. Historically, this is the method that I have used most often and is the one I prefer. Effectively, you manage the project. You lead all communication with the client. You'll probably set up a meeting with your client and your business partner. This is when all the key interested parties get to meet each other. This may mean that you need to brief your business partner in advance. This might be on the phone or it could be in the car on the way to the client meeting. Clearly, this will work best if you are presenting a united front to your new prospective client. So, ultimately you must feel that you can trust your sub-contract partner to deal directly with YOUR client.

It also means that you retain a complete commercial relationship with the client. You organise the invoicing. The way I have worked with business partners in the past has been that we have agreed that I pay them once I get paid. That way, you protect your business *and* safeguard your cashflow. And of course, if your new business partner is happy to agree to this, then you have something you can both work to. I have never had an issue working this way. Doing it this way round means that you have more to do. But it also means that you manage the relationship with your client. You are thereby protecting this relationship, making it less likely that you will lose the client in the future.

My other recommendation is to allow your business partner or subcontractor to set their own fee. I have always had this relationship with people I have worked with collaboratively. They can set their fee to be whatever they want. They must of course bear in mind that you will add a mark-up on top before you go to the client. Therefore, it is not in their interests to be too greedy, as the risk is that you won't land the business. Similarly, if they are in the habit of generally putting in prices which are high, they also jeopardise the relationship with you because you may of course exercise your right to find another provider who is more price competitive. So, it works well because it is self-policing.

The reason I have tended to use this model though is that, as I have always explained to my collaborative partners, I don't want them to undertake a job representing me and my business whilst resenting the work. If I've screwed them down on price just to get the deal, and they're not doing it enthusiastically, then it's a false economy. Nevertheless, I've always had an open relationship to the extent that, if I feel we need to revisit our price in order to land a particular piece of business, or I think that what the client is asking for is reasonable, I will of course go back to my partner. They have the chance at that point to decide whether they are interested in taking the work at this fee. Hopefully, working this way benefits all parties.

The other benefit of working collaboratively with people is that you may end up obtaining work leads and referrals from them as well. Indeed, you may feel that if both of you are likely to generate a similar amount of business for each other that you simply swap leads. You do not necessarily have to agree to make any commission payments at all. It is completely up to you. Nevertheless, you can see how building up a network of like-minded people can help both you and them, whilst keeping the competition out.

Finally, the very fact that you are mixing, meeting, and talking to another businessperson who operates in a synergistic way to you, can be beneficial. You can swap ideas and get advice from each other. You can't put a value on the quality of these types of relationships.

Remember though the key benefit about working this way is that it means you can say *"yes"* more often and *"no"* less often. Both these things are particularly important.

2. Methodical approach to sales activity

It is tempting to hope that one day you will wake up and think of a way of selling that no one has ever thought of before. And I wish you the best of luck with that. However, what is much more realistic is that we stand as much chance of becoming a pioneer in selling as we do of becoming multi-millionaires on the lottery. Of course, it can be an aspiration, but you probably need to get on with doing something more practical in the meantime. *This comes from doing the basics right.* It comes from doing the hard yards and doing them consistently. Find out what works, and just keep doing it. Day in, day out, relentlessly, just keep doing it. The best way of working out an effective way of selling is to look at the habits and behaviour of other successful salespeople. Watch what they do and copy the process. Sure, you may need to adapt it to suit your personality. We're all different after all. But certain things work for a reason. So, it makes sense to just learn and practise them.

Much of this is common sense. But as Charlie Mullins, the chief executive of Pimlico Plumbers, once famously said, *"The problem is common sense ain't that common."* So, this means being organised. Have a plan for how you're going to grow your sales. It involves doing some pre-call preparation, whether on the phone or going to see somebody face to face. It means keeping comprehensive and diligent notes. They don't have to be lengthy, but they need to have all the key things you want to know about this customer and their buying habits. Work your systems and keep them updated regularly. I know that for many natural born salespeople, keeping on top of the admin isn't their favourite job in the world. And that may be understandable, but it doesn't alter the fact that those who are organised and structured are more likely to be successful. So, it's your choice!

Record-keeping

For me, this methodical approach to selling is partly about trying to understand the process as much as possible. As I mentioned in the last chapter, I keep a record of the call result each time I complete a prospecting call. I use a rudimentary tick box system for this. I also keep a record of the number of decision makers I get through to. These of course are the only useful calls that you make.

The frustrating bit is that you must make all the other calls just to uncover these gold nuggets. These are your opportunities. It doesn't matter how good a salesperson you are, if you make 22 calls in a row and you are unable to get through to anybody that you could sell to, then you have no chance of selling.

I also monitor the amount of business I win related to the amount of time I spend on the phone. This creates an effectiveness ratio. I'm not suggesting that you should necessarily work in the same way, but for me, this is an important part of my personal organisation.

3. Belief

As mentioned earlier, you need to believe in the products or services that you sell. In selling, you're interacting with other human beings and therefore if you don't believe in it why should they? You're also having these conversations with somebody without any input from another human being. Unless you have set up call recording, you are on your own. In fact, I'm amazed by the number of companies who still don't have call recording in place. Far from being a 'spy in the cab', it is a great aid to sales training and to being able to analyse ways in which a sales conversation could be improved, or to find subtle cues from the client which you missed during the call.

So, it is important to feel motivated by a strong belief in your offering and your message on every call you make. Top TV presenters are not necessarily the most knowledgeable people in their sector. However, the reason they get paid big bucks to present to us is that they have a way of communicating to us positively and enthusiastically.

I've always felt that Rick Stein, Jamie Oliver and Brian Cox are very watchable because they clearly love what they do.

4. Mental toughness

I have observed, over the years, that successful salespeople tend to be tough mentally. They tend not to be wallflowers or shrinking violets. Let's consider why this is important in sales. The very nature of doing a sales job means that you are opening yourself up to other human beings rejecting you. Every day, you try to get somebody interested in something. They always have the option of letting you down by saying, *"No, I'm not interested."*

This goes against everything that our subconscious mind wants to hear. We want to be accepted. We want to be loved. We want people to like us. I am not sure that the majority of people ever change from this, as it is deep-rooted in our psyche. But what successful salespeople do is to learn to cope with it. They learn not to take it personally, and they learn not to let it put them off their stride. It is important to remember in selling that the person is not rejecting you personally. They are simply rejecting what you are putting to them now, today. This could mean that they could say yes to the same thing tomorrow. Or it could mean that they could say yes to something else, just not the thing that you've just asked them about. So, the word 'No' should be seen as something quite short term, and specific. As you can tell, this requires a fair amount of positive thought. Again, this is something you generally find in most successful salespeople. They believe in possibilities, and they believe in themselves. These are glass half-full, not glass half-empty kind of people. They are largely optimists.

I believe that

> *"Everyone is a customer, it's just that some of them haven't bought from you yet."*

Think long term, and always try to see the bigger picture. Always base your contact strategy with the prospective client on what you believe the business potential to be, rather than the relationship you have with the person. Let me explain.

Example – Prospect A

You talk to them periodically, and you get on well with the decision-maker. He's a genuinely nice person and always spends time chatting to you. He supports the same football team as you and has other similar interests to you. You would guess he's a similar age to you.

His company is on the edge of the type of industry you typically work with, and so they spend around £100 twice a year on your types of products.

This is the one to bin of course, or at least reduce activity on. By all means connect on LinkedIn. Have him as a distant connection if you want, but don't spend masses of sales time on this account.

Example – Prospect B

This one is completely different. This is quite a big company, and they consume a lot of the products that you can supply. Nevertheless, the decision maker doesn't seem particularly keen to engage with you, and he's told you clearly that they are quite happy using another supplier. They benefit from good prices from them and furthermore their sales contact is a member of the same golf club. On the face of it, this is the one that you should patiently pursue. Keep knocking on the door.

There is potential in this prospect company and that's the reason you should maintain contact, even if you don't particularly like the person that you deal with. One day something will change. They could potentially have a falling out with their current supplier, or their current supplier ends up letting them down. Perhaps they're out of stock on some of their products. Who is that prospect now most likely to turn to? Their next best alternative, which is you of course!

I'm a big believer that there can be prizes for being second in selling, but I'll cover that elsewhere.

STORIES FROM THE FRONT

In the early days of running my training business I contacted a company in Loughborough, North Leicestershire. I had identified them as a prospective client because they had been advertising for an internal sales position. Internal sales, along with telesales, telemarketing and customer service phone-based roles, are fertile ground for my training consultancy business. However, the contact that I got through to was not especially helpful. He did tell me enough to indicate that they did all their training in-house and that it worked successfully. As far as he was concerned there was no reason why they would ever need to look at an external training provider such as me.

I tried to keep in touch, over a period of 18 months. Then, on one occasion when I called to speak to him, I was told that he had left. The new contact, Kevin, was open and seemed keen to do things differently. He was also keen to understand what I could do to support them and their plans for developing the business in the future. I went to meet him, and as I am sure you have guessed, they turned into a significant client for me in the early days of my business. I learned an important lesson. Don't give up on a company just because somebody tries to shut the door on you. If you believe that the company's application means that they should be suitable for your range of products or services, then try to keep in touch.

5. Ambition

Commission payments, bonuses and incentives are clear evidence that good employers recognise that good salespeople will typically be ambitious. They offer these financial incentives to attract the best quality people. As I'm sure you're aware, some of these payments can be massive. By and large, successful salespeople will be the type of people who want a better holiday next year than they had this year, and this year they hope to have a better holiday than last year. They want a flashier car, and they want to live in a better neighbourhood. And I'm not criticising any of these things. In fact, it's necessary for salespeople to be ambitious because that's what gets them out of bed in the morning.

I've observed over the years that successful salespeople have a strong work ethic too. They will typically be focused & highly organised. Mentally at least. This still doesn't extend to a love of administration though. The day doesn't finish at 5. There is frequently paperwork and admin to do once the enjoyable part of the working day is done. Again, I'm not saying this is a good or a bad thing, it's just that I notice it seems to go with the territory. Successful people are ambitious and want to keep on achieving more and more. Most of the time, the customer interaction is one-to-one, and so therefore the salesperson needs to believe that this transaction could help improve their own life directly.

6. Good interpersonal skills

These are important too. In sales you're selling to humans, so clearly your ability to get on with them is important. If you like people, this all helps too. A successful salesperson will frequently be somebody who is happy chatting to people, and willing to try and build relationships with strangers. Their social skills are likely to be advanced.

I have the greatest respect for salespeople who seem to have that natural ability to get on with anybody. You can drop them into any social or work situation, and they have a blend of skills which makes people warm to them. Naturally. They seem to be popular. Some of them may admittedly be larger-than-life characters, who clearly always want to be the centre of attention. I have worked with and met many of these types of people over the years. I'm sure you have too. But not all successful salespeople are necessarily the 'life and soul.'

When done well, this all looks like an entirely natural process. In fact, it takes considerable work and skill. People may appear to have a natural ability to relate to other people, but consciously or subconsciously they have simply developed highly fine-tuned antennae. To be natural with anybody means that you must be good at working out what type of person you are dealing with, and what type of communication they want from you. If you are selling to a group of people who are quite different from you, you clearly must learn how that group of individuals generally operates. Plus, a fair degree of empathy needs to go on here. Watching a young nurse communicating with an elderly patient can often be a great example of empathy. You may sell to a customer base that is a completely different age to you. Alternatively, you may sell to a group of people who are in a distinct social category or class. Think, for example, of the person in the Bentley or Lamborghini showroom. Good interpersonal skills are therefore an integral part of being a successful salesperson.

7. Good communication skills

I train teams of people for a living, and therefore you might expect this to be on my list. Nevertheless, I hope it goes without saying that good communication skills are essential to good selling. Good patient listening, good use of vocal tone, and good questioning techniques are part of the armoury you need when communicating with customers.

The ability to be able to convey ideas in a simple and yet enthusiastic way is clearly important. There are some industries where this takes on a particular significance. Consider if you sell in a technical environment, IT for instance. Or the car industry perhaps. In each of these cases, it's important that your communication skills can communicate potentially complex subjects in an easily digestible form. This may take considerable patience, and in many cases I find that it also means the technical person has developed examples and analogies as a way of explaining things.

STORIES FROM THE FRONT

I remember years ago when IT was just getting started. I'm talking about the mid-80s. Prior to that, any form of storage system was based on paper, and generally handwritten. Customer cards were usually on pre-printed forms or paper which the salesperson simply filled in or ticked boxes with a pen. Many field-based sales teams used these sales cards. With the very first telemarketing team that I managed, every customer conversation was recorded in writing on a pre-printed paper form. Given that we had a team of 6 telemarketers, each making more than 100 calls a day, this required us to have an admin team of two simply to keep all the paper moving. When I look back at it now, I wonder how we managed.

Our management team realised that computers would do a far more effective job of storing all this information.

We appointed a computer bureau in Basildon, Essex, who worked with us to develop the software that each telemarketer was to use on a screen at their desk. We also paid them a subscription service for storing all our data. I remember in one meeting a question coming up about the difference between the size of the hard drive and RAM. I sense some of you glazing over already! However, I remember their marketing director Martyn explaining the difference to us something like this. He said, *"Imagine that your data is held in a library. Well, the size of that library equates to the size of your hard drive. So, the more customer records you develop over the next few years, the bigger the hard drive we will need to be able to store it. Now the RAM is all to do with speed, so it's a reference to how quickly you can take out the books that you want from your library."* Now that little off-the-cuff definition has always stayed with me. I was impressed with how the marketing director in a technical environment found a way to explain a concept to us in a way that we could all relate to. I guess that being the marketing director, he had a blend of technical skills, but also appreciated how his customer thinks.

Regardless of how we view ourselves in the above 7 areas, all of us can improve our sales skills. In the main, following set procedures in your approach to selling will yield improved results. This can be learned by adopting the practices of many successful salespeople. There are many, many books published on the secret, or not so secret, ways of selling. This book is not intended to tread that well-worn path. Instead, it is intended to cover some of the things that will help you on the phone when you're making outbound business calls.

Chapter summary

To be a successful salesperson requires a blend of skills that we all have naturally, to a greater or lesser extent. It is about fine-tuning these to develop the approach that works with each specific customer or prospect. And of course, the method that works with one person may not necessarily work with the next. That's all part of the fun! Oh yes, and frustration too on occasion!

Treat it as a profession and appreciate that the skills need working on. Every day in every transaction with customers we can all learn a little more. Some things work. Some things don't. But that's not just selling, that's life in general. So, don't be too hard on yourself! Just think about what works when people sell to you and observe other successful people around you. You can learn a huge amount.

We'll come back to the structure of the sales process in Chapter 8. In the meantime, though, let's consider what is required of you.

CHAPTER 3:

BEING A NICE PERSON

This chapter is all about you. It's about your role in building the relationship with your customer. When thinking about your approach to any of your existing customers or potential prospects, it's easy to focus on the product or service that you are going to talk to them about. This is important, clearly. However, my view is that this isn't the most important thing. **The most important thing is YOU.** Yes, you're selling your product or service of course. But you're also selling yourself. Every time you interact with your customer, you are selling yourself, and the business or organisation that you represent. If you're employed, this is of course your company. However, if you're self-employed then your business is you.

Consider the situation from the customer's point of view as well. The product or service that they sign up to buy from you will matter to them. It needs to do the job. It needs to give good results. However, the chances are that in most markets what they buy from you, they could probably buy elsewhere. Therefore, when they make the purchase decision with you, they also invest in a relationship with you and your company. They want to feel that they can trust you, and that you will look after them.

In B2B relationships particularly, frequently both parties are looking to establish a long-term trading relationship. Therefore of course they want to feel that you are the right person for them to trade with. Your customer wants to be treated fairly, and they want to know that if things go wrong (which they inevitably will at some point), you will support them.

Looking back

When I look back at my career, I believe I have always tried to do this: to be nice to others in my working life. And this is long before I got involved in selling my own business to new customers. Before that, in the days when I was employed, the people I interacted with were all internal and so I never dealt with customers. However, my impulse to be nice was still there then.

Hardly a revolutionary tip for me to offer you is it?

Clearly my parents must take most of the credit for this. This is mainly to do with how I was brought up. In a middle-class area in west London, I was taught to respect others and to respect myself. In turn, I believe that my parents also demonstrated the same behaviour. Whilst they were different personalities, both Mum and Dad acted in ways that meant I could always trust them.

Given that I'm not trying to preach to you, or write a book on parenting, we'll park this and move on. Nevertheless, treating your customers in the way that you like to be treated by everyone else is a reasonable blueprint for what will make you successful in sales.

It's all about the relationship you have with them. I had just such an experience early on after I'd set up my business.

STORIES FROM THE FRONT

A few months after I started trading, I uncovered a new prospect in the eastern counties. This company was a software house which specialised in developing tools and enhancing what was a leading software product at the time.

I went to see them, and even before I got out of the car I was impressed with the set-up. They worked in a slightly rural location, working out of a converted barn. It all looked very swanky. They were clearly doing well. I got on well with the contact Steve, and the business potential looked particularly good. He told me that they were looking for two courses. That's 2 two-day courses. When you're self-employed and in the early days, you inevitably focus on how you are going to pay for the food and roof over your head. Consequently, I felt particularly good on the 45-minute drive back home to my office.

I sent a quote to Steve a couple of days later, having decided that I could make reasonable money out of this project. This client company was clearly successful and growing rapidly. I was ecstatic to land the business a week or so later. We booked the training, and I turned up on site to deliver four days of sales training to their international team of bright young things over a couple of weeks. I enjoyed working with them. I made sure that I spent some time with Steve while I was on site, and he also introduced me to his general manager, Andrea. I kept in touch with him, and always felt that we got on well. This was a great account because I managed to generate more business with them too.

On one occasion after completing a piece of training work, Steve mentioned to me that he had landed a promotion. He was off to be the general manager of the subsidiary company in Japan. I congratulated him. This certainly seemed like a good opportunity for him to develop his career. In a successful, rapidly growing company, there is always the likelihood of star performers being moved around. And I suspect Steve was a star performer.

From that day, I never had another piece of work from that company. It's one of the lessons I learned - that it's so much about the strength of the relationship that the two of you have. The potential that client had for sales training never changed. They still had a telephone-based international sales team. Some people moved on, others joined. I kept in touch with the new contacts over a period of years, by phoning them periodically. Unfortunately for me, the general manager Andrea who had spoken highly of my training and thanked me for the work I'd done, also moved on. The best two contacts I had within the company at senior level were both out of the frame within a relatively short space of time.

> However, I never got anything out of the replacement decision-makers. They didn't know me and they had their own way of doing things. Presumably, they wanted to do things differently, as 'new brooms' often do, and for me that was it!

This principle can work for you, and it can work against you. It's all part of the ebb and flow of sales.

Polite persistence pays

So, if you find yourself in a similar situation, don't despair - it will often work in your favour too of course. There may be accounts you are trying to break into, where they clearly have a good relationship with their sales contact. As far as you are concerned, you have no opportunity to break into this business currently. Nevertheless, it is worth keeping in periodic contact. Polite persistence pays, as one client, David, told me when I finally landed a piece of work with his company. I'd never heard that phrase before.

It is highly likely that the customer is loyal to one of your competitors because they feel they are being well looked after. It is quite probable that their product or service is no better than yours. However, you can't make any headway because the customer feels that they don't need to consider alternatives. They're happy as they are.

Then one day your competitor's salesperson leaves the company. This is always quite likely, because somebody successful will frequently be ambitious, or will be poached by other companies. Now it is open season. Your potential customer will now be likely to review their options and look at the market. You now have your opportunity. If you've kept in touch with them, and they've got to know you a little, even at arms-length, then you are well positioned.

We're always brought up with the maxim, "There are no prizes for second." Certainly, in the competitive world of sport, we are far less likely to remember the runners-up. We may remember consistent winners such as Usain Bolt or Mo Farah, but we are likely to struggle to name those who won the silver or bronze medals in those epic races. The same with the Grand National. The same with the World Cup or FA Cup finals. You get the point. The ultimate legacy comes from winning things, not from finishing second.

There are prizes for second in sales

I believe strongly that in sales at least, there ARE prizes for second. If you can't be number one, aim to be number two. One day your chance will come. As I've just mentioned, the preferred supplier's sales contact may well leave at some point. Alternatively, there may be one occasion when your prospect can't get hold of a product from their supplier. They will turn to the person who they consider offers them the next best option. This is your opportunity to impress them with what you can do. Even if you've only won one small order, you've nevertheless created a chink in the armour of your competitor. You have dealt a significant blow because you now have a trading relationship with this customer and the opportunity and reason to engage in dialogue with them.

What type of person do you need to be?

Let's start with the importance of being an authentic version of you. If you're acting naturally when interacting with your customers, clearly this will be easier for you than if it's something which is forced. Putting on an act is tiring, and chances are the customer will see through it anyway.

Be honest and understand that personal integrity is paramount. Of course, being honest must be mixed with a modicum of common sense. Being brutally honest, where for instance you end up blaming other work colleagues for things which haven't happened, isn't constructive behaviour. Therefore, approaching communication with customers positively will be more effective than being blunt.

However, personal integrity is incredibly important. As I mentioned earlier, for the customer to decide they want to trade with you, they must feel that they can trust you, and that it is worth building a relationship with you. They are also emotionally investing in the relationship with you, just as you are with them.

STORIES FROM THE FRONT

In my early days of trading, I set up my business account with the bank I'd had my personal account with for many years, Barclays. In those days they used to have business bankers who operated from their branches. I was new to business banking, and grateful for any help or guidance I could get. I received a call, inviting me in to meet my business manager. I met a smart guy wearing a suit, in the offices upstairs. A hallowed part of the bank I'd never seen before.

I was slightly disappointed with the meeting, as I didn't get the impression he knew much about small businesses. He seemed like a corporate man through and through. He started the meeting well though, asking me questions about me and the business. However, he then went into sales mode, and tried to sell me some of the many products that were on offer. He completely misread what I was there for, and I lost interest.

About three to four months later, I received another call from the bank telling me that the business manager had now changed. The guy I had met previously had moved on to another role and, *"Would you like to come in and meet his new replacement?"* For me as the customer this was a simple question to answer. *"No"* was my response. You see, I had invested some time and effort in trying to build a relationship with the person I had been to meet. However, this new request made me realise that all the people in these roles were going through revolving doors, so I couldn't see the point in having a personal relationship with anyone at the bank. Ultimately of course these roles disappeared. Presumably, they weren't adding much value, and when the financial crash happened in 2008, things changed. I can't say I was surprised.

Treating customers and prospects equally

I also recommend keeping in regular touch with your customers and your prospects. Have you noticed that the best relationships you have with friends socially are those who you communicate with most frequently? Most of my customer interaction is on the telephone of course. I try to keep in regular contact with current customers. It's important not to ignore them simply because business is going well. Your business with them is always vulnerable. It may be that someone else is working harder to try and win the account. Keep in touch and ask them how their business is going. It's not prescriptive and therefore you need to make your own decisions about the frequency of contact. I generally always finish a call by agreeing with the customer when I will contact them next. Hopefully, that way, your frequency of contact with them will be about right. Clearly, contacting them too frequently will irritate them, and will be counterproductive. Conversely, if you leave it too long, chances are you may miss something. So just like the three bears' porridge, it needs to achieve that Goldilocks' balance: not too hot, not too cold, just right.

I use the same contact strategy with new prospective customers. I don't call them more frequently than current customers, in a desperate attempt to win their business. But then neither do I call them less frequently. My view is that each case must be considered in isolation. Furthermore, within my own database, I don't even distinguish between customers or prospects. I treat them all the same. I remember who my customers are when I'm calling them, but there is no flag or marker against live trading accounts in my contact database.

The next thing to consider is how you are going to open your call. I will cover this in the chapter on *Structuring the Sales Call*.

Being human

Another aspect of establishing a good relationship with a prospective customer is that you need to demonstrate that you are a human being. Ultimately, if they're going to forge a relationship with you, it's you the person who the relationship is with. Of course, your company's branding and image is important in how it supports you, but your contact with them is the key link.

You are a unique human, made up of many different characteristics. You have your foibles and idiosyncrasies. There are certain things that you are exceptionally good at. And maybe some things you're perhaps not so good at.

It's important that over time you reveal this non-work-related element of your life. This will help you build rapport. You do need to be selective though. I am aware that with any tips or advice I offer, you need to apply it to the person you are dealing with. No two situations, and certainly no two customers, are the same. You may well have some customers in your portfolio who clearly require your relationship with them to be strictly transactional. They don't want any chat; they don't want to be friends with you. They just want you to provide them with the product or service that they require, in the shortest possible time and in the easiest way. Respect that and work with it. Don't try to persuade them to be your best friend.

For instance, if I'm dealing with somebody from my bank on the telephone, I'm not that interested in them personally. I don't need to know what football team they support, and I don't want to know how many children they have. I just want to complete my banking transaction accurately, and in the shortest possible time. The reason for this of course is that chances are I will never speak to them again.

There can be no hard and fast rules here. Over time though you will probably gradually release more information about yourself. If your main communication is with them on the telephone, if you are a telesales or telemarketing agent for instance, you will probably have less opportunity to do this. Alternatively, if you are a field-based representative, and you spend longer with each customer sat with them face-to-face, you have far more opportunity to work on the social side of your relationship.

Feel free to talk about other outside interests you have. You may chat to them about members of your family. You may have hobbies that they will remember you for. To some degree you are building your personal brand. If it gets you remembered and helps you stand out from the competition, then so much the better. So, to some degree, the quirkier the better! I often find that when you meet somebody socially, the conversation will often start with you both trying to find things you have in common. Once you've managed to achieve this, the relationship generally gets easier to build. It might be something very general such as the fact that you are both dog owners. Alternatively, it could be some hobby that you both have in common. You might both support the same team. You might both wear the same brand of unusual shoes.

Incidentally, this one really happened. Years ago, I went to a presentation at a bank branch. The speaker was wearing a particularly smart pair of men's shoes. They were slightly unusual, but I didn't take a lot of notice other than noticing that he was smartly dressed. However, one of the guys in the audience did take a lot more notice because seemingly he was a big fan of the same brand. So, he went up to the speaker after he'd given his talk and complimented him on his shoes. They got into an enthusiastic and earnest conversation about that specific brand. True story. These things happen.

You will often be surprised who remembers what about you. I have an interest in cocktails and cocktail making, and a secondary business where we provide cocktails for people in their homes. This is of course an unusual hobby and completely different to my day job. I will frequently forget that this has come up in conversation, but people will ask me about it either on the phone or if I'm sat with them. I have one client, Simon, who I did some training work for years ago. I generally speak to him about once every 18 months or so, but he always asks me about it. He will say towards the end of our conversation, *"and how's the cocktail business going?"* This is nice, as it means that this other human being remembers me for something specific and personal.

I also organise a lads' weekend away in the autumn each year. This is something we've been doing for many years and involves cycling. We choose some fantastic and picturesque parts of Britain to cycle around, and typically we cycle about 120 miles over three days. We literally cycle over hills and dales. I have another client in the eastern counties who I've been fortunate enough to carry out a large amount of work with over the last few years. He and his company treat me well, and we have a good relationship. Generally, when we meet up to talk about training, he will schedule the meeting so that he can take me for lunch. This is unusual, but much appreciated! We talk about the state of the nation, football (he's an Ipswich Town fan), and of course his team at work and his company's performance. Nevertheless, he will generally ask me how my cycling is going. He's not a cyclist himself, but he still has an interest in my activity and our cycling weekends. It's great when you can forge these types of relationships. They will generally always be business led and it's important to remember that you are there to support them and their business. But there's nothing wrong in having a bit of social chit-chat on the side.

Always keep it positive though. If your contact is a similar age to you, with children of a similar age, you might compare notes on how you coped with young children and home schooling during the coronavirus pandemic. You may describe that as a challenge. But you don't want to share this morning's row with your partner. That's off limits. Keeping things light and positive is key.

Take an interest in them

Just as it's useful for you to let them into elements of your life where appropriate, you will gain massive wins if you take an interest in them. The reasoning doesn't need explaining. They will warm to you instantly if they feel that you are interested in them as a person. This will be considerably easier where you have an interest in something that they're really keen on. Or if not a keen interest, at least some knowledge about it.

30 years ago, I went to see somebody working at the British Aerospace plant in Filton, near Bristol. I noticed as I walked into his office that he had pictures up on the wall that indicated he was actively involved in mountaineering and hill-walking. I have no specialist knowledge about this, but my late father did. He used to be a mountaineering instructor. This gave me the opportunity to ask this prospective customer about his mountaineering. I asked him where he liked to go, and it allowed me to talk briefly about some of the things that I know my dad had done in the past. Then of course when I used to speak to him afterwards on the telephone, for a period of time, I would often ask him if he'd been anywhere interesting recently climbing mountains.

There are many things you can do to help you with this. You can make a note in your desk diary, or at the very least lock it away in your head. There are now laws around what personal information you can store about people but knowing something about a particular hobby or interest that they have is unlikely to get you into trouble, I hope.

There are some additional useful ways of reinforcing the fact that you are thinking about them. You may see an article on one of their industry's websites. If you think it would be relevant or of interest to them, why not simply email it across to them? Send it with a brief note which simply says something like, *"I saw this and thought of you. I hope it is of interest."* You can also signpost people to articles on LinkedIn. If their company has recently won an industry award, then again it is a great idea to drop them a note to congratulate them.

I carried out some work for a period of years supporting the board of directors of a rapidly growing family-owned logistics and warehousing company. I would frequently send them articles about anything I thought would help their business. This would even include forthcoming seminars on changing HR legislation. I sent this directly to the HR manager. All these activities will indicate to the people you deal with that you are thinking of them and have their best interests at heart. Of course, you're trying to sell to them, and they will always know that. But nevertheless, there is plenty you can do that demonstrates you're looking to build a proper professional working relationship with them. And for me this goes way beyond the selling activity.

Be informed

It's also useful to be well-informed. Informed about a broad range of things that control all our lives. This helps you to develop relationships with people you work with. They are part of the business community, as you are, and so they will have thoughts and opinions about things that affect them personally and their business in general.

Therefore, I suggest that you do need to have an up-to-date understanding of what's going on in the news more widely. This will include some elements of political understanding too, I'm afraid. Now if this really isn't you, and you are simply not interested in politics at all, then ignore it and move on. I have said elsewhere that part of being an effective salesperson is to be authentic. True to yourself.

So, don't swot up on politics if it isn't ever going to interest you. However, demonstrating a reasonably detailed grasp of current affairs is a great indicator that you are the sort of person who can listen, take in knowledge and respond to different circumstances, all the sorts of things that a good salesperson does when helping customers.

I should stress that I suggest being informed. This is different to having an opinion. Clearly, you need to be careful about not expressing too strong an opinion, particularly around things such as politics. Your views may be the complete opposite to your customer. And this clearly isn't going to help! You might think that the prime minister of the day is a complete idiot and responsible for most of the things that are going wrong with the country. But if your customer respects them deeply and thinks they're doing a fantastic job in difficult times, there is almost certainly no way the two of you are going to reconcile your views. In this instance, you need to be relaxed about your viewpoint and avoid getting into any discussion on this topic with your customer. So, be informed, not opinionated.

As mentioned above, both you and your customer are part of a business community. Therefore, you will benefit from having some basic understanding of what's going on business-wise. There may be business events coming up. You and your company might specialise in selling to specific industry sectors. Clearly, in this instance it is useful to understand what's going on in that sector. Education is a good example of this. If your products or services are sold principally to schools and other education establishments, then clearly it helps to know what's going on. Government policy inevitably affects spending in this area. Changes to the curriculum may also make a difference to your business opportunities. The growth of academies too may impact your business. So, in these examples it makes sense to understand the industry, and the likely impact of any changes.

A bit of reading around the subject will clearly help you. Hopefully, this is something that you are interested in, but if not, it's still worth reading a few articles and posts on social media. However, I should point out that it's facts you're after, not somebody simply having a rant on Twitter.

In summary, the advice is to be informed and make sure you're up to date. Know what's going on in politics and life in general. This all demonstrates that you're a rounded human being. Other people will respond to you better if they feel you have a bit of personality and depth of character. Nevertheless, it's important to always keep it light, and positive. Nobody wants to hear you ranting. This is because they want to know that you are the type of person who can help them do things better and help improve their business. If you come across as being negative, they are more likely to mistrust you and feel that you will rush to blame everybody when things go wrong.

Be business-like

I have just given my thoughts on what we might consider are the softer parts of the business relationship. But in equal measure it's also important to be both professional and business-like. On occasions, this means being hard-headed. Perhaps an 'iron-fist in a velvet glove.'

So, this means saying *"No"* sometimes. I think the word 'no' is an underrated part of our ability to be effective.

We are all brought up with the notion that *'the customer is always right.'* Fundamentally, I don't believe in this philosophy. I respect it and I do appreciate where it comes from. Nevertheless, the people you deal with as customers and prospects are of course human beings, the same as you. Sometimes, they will try to pull a fast one. They may not always be completely truthful. Sometimes this may be accidental, or it could be a calculated move on their part.

I'm from a marketing background, and therefore I understand that the customer is at the centre of the relationship we have with them. Their needs are paramount, and we must do everything we can to support them. That is our responsibility, both professionally and as human beings. Equally importantly though, we also need to know where to draw the line. You have a responsibility to your customer of course, but equally you have a responsibility to your company or organisation. And of course, if it's your business, then that responsibility is to yourself.

Consequently, you are often in a situation where you need to make judgment calls. It may be that the customer is making demands of you and your company. And it could be that they are in a pickle, because of something they've done or not done. You want to do what you possibly can to help, and sometimes this may involve swallowing some pride. Equally though, on occasions you need to be assertive and let them know positively that you're not able to give them everything they want at this time.

You may want to help them out by doing them a favour. There's nothing wrong in reinforcing the fact that this is a one-off gesture on your part. You are underlining the fact that you can't necessarily do the same thing for them in the future in the same situation.

Being successful in sales, often involves being tenacious. A sale doesn't always come to the person who most deserves it. It is a competitive environment generally, and therefore we need to be organised and steal a march on anyone else trying to pitch for the same business.

STORIES FROM THE FRONT

Back in the late '90s, I worked in the truck rental industry. A company offered me a job to oversee all their direct marketing. They had never run a telephone-based team. Nevertheless, they recognised the potential of having a well-organised outbound telemarketing unit. I think this is a large part of why the managing director offered me the job. I started by recruiting a small team of four people and one of them, Michael, was a bit of a pain to manage. A nice enough lad, but he took chances and cut corners when he could. He was young, only 19, and keen to get on in life. Nevertheless, the image he created for himself very quickly within the company was of being a loud, brash wide-boy. Two managers of neighbouring departments close to our open plan offices told me informally that they were not impressed by him. They weren't heavy about it, and they weren't quite telling me what to do. Nevertheless, it was quite clear that if he was to be working for them, he would be skating on thin ice.

I spent a fair bit of management time with Michael and felt that we achieved considerable success. Although in the early days many of my conversations with him were gentle reprimands, over time we ended up with what I believe was strong mutual respect. He became a valued asset to my team. He was tenacious and became the highest achieving member of that telemarketing team. Another interesting by-product of his high performance was that over time this started to increase the performance of the other members of the team around him. They had all been there longer than him. They had worked out all the reasons why they weren't able to achieve any more results than they were getting. But Michael joined and pretty much blew their excuses out of the water. There was a large logistics company based in Scotland where Michael was keen to get hold of the decision maker. However, whenever he called the man he needed to speak to, he was unavailable. He was either in a meeting, or at another depot or on holiday. And this was in the good old days before people started rejecting cold calls! We had office hours of 8-6, with the phone team working from 8:30-5. Michael didn't give up on this account and started staying on at work so that he could phone the guy just before 6:00pm, or at 8:15 or 8:20 in the morning. And guess what? He eventually managed to get hold of him. His reward was that he managed to secure us some business. This was with a company that we'd never worked with previously. So, this was a new account. A fantastic achievement. I can't quite remember whether this account amounted to much. I don't think it did, but that's the way it rolls sometimes.

Nevertheless, it was Michael's tenacity that managed to land this piece of business. Then, after about six months, he walked into my office one morning and passed me that plain white envelope. I knew what was coming! He was ambitious and wanted to get on. He went off to join a recruitment company. I don't know what happened to him from there, as we lost touch.

Persistence pays off

So, be determined with people on the phone when you feel the situation deserves it. For example, you might be following up a proposal that you've prepared for somebody. You've probably spent a fair bit of time on it and, after all, they asked you for it, or at least agreed for you to do the work. If you are a salesperson out in the field, or it is your own business, you will probably have been to see them as well. So that's your time and fuel. Morally, I believe you have a right to at least get a response from them about their views on your proposal.

You may find that once you've sent the proposal, the trail goes cold. I don't believe that people ignore you in order to be rude. I'm always happy to give them the benefit of the doubt. However, if you cannot get hold of them on the first or second follow-up call, it's fine to consider another series of tactics to make contact.

I suggest that you need to consider a diverse range of contact methods. Presumably, if you've written them a proposal, you consider that there is likely to be some business to be had. So, these opportunities are worth pursuing. One thing you can do is send them an email. I would generally keep this fairly light and refer to the fact that you've contacted them a couple of times by phone, and that you appreciate they're busy. You go on to say that you are following up the proposal, and that you're keen to know what their current thinking is. I would generally recommend your email finishes with a line such as, *"I look forward to hearing from you."* This is your attempt to put the ball in their court. Hopefully, they'll contact you. Sometimes it works, sometimes it doesn't.

Alternatively, you could contact them through your LinkedIn connection. Sometimes people find it easier to send a short message back through LinkedIn than they do to write an email. This occasionally works for me, and so it might work for you. How about sending them a letter in the post? This reinforces your professionalism and makes the communication more formal. It is also a tangible demonstration of your effort and focus on their behalf. Receiving a business letter is so rare now that it will certainly get noticed!

Frequently, I find that the reason people don't contact you back or are unavailable to talk to is that nothing much has happened on their side. Perhaps they've given the proposal to their boss, or they're trying to fix up a meeting. But for whatever reason, it's just not happened yet. They have nothing material to tell you at this point. That's got to be a strong reason for anybody to put off contacting you. However, until you know this for sure you're in a state of limbo. Certainly, you don't want to leave this prospect out there until they are ready to move. You may well end up missing out on the business, so you need to try and stay close and track the progress of your proposal or quote with them.

Depending on what sort of relationship you have with this person, and with the company, another option is to try and talk to somebody else in their team. Maybe you have previously spoken to their boss, or you already know them. If you try unsuccessfully, on repeated occasions, to get hold of Paul, why not ask to go through to his boss Sarah? You have little to lose by doing this. Ultimately Paul may not be happy that you've gone above his head, but if you've tried to contact him on various occasions and left numerous messages, he is unlikely to complain too much.

You may also aim to contact people in other departments – who at the very least may know what's going on with the project. For instance, if you deal with somebody in maintenance or manufacturing, and your proposal is part of a much bigger plan, there will inevitably be other people in the company who can give you the inside track. For me selling training, I may deal with the sales manager or the customer service manager. But if I can't get hold of them, chances are that somebody in HR or in Learning and Development will at least know something about what's going on with any training plans. In fact, frequently they hold the budget, so ultimately any decisions about training need to be done with their involvement and consent in any case.

Some are more equal than others

There will be some people you deal with who you want to make feel special. These could be some of your important regular customers. You may also want to single out those people who have placed large orders with you. Additionally, there will be other people who you would very much like to win over. These are your key prospects. It goes without saying that we should treat everybody equally. Everyone responds better in these situations. However, and this is not a contradiction, there will be some people who you will want to ensure understand that you value and appreciate their business.

These may be the people who you look to treat slightly differently on occasions. There are many ways you can build rapport with this group of valuable customers and prospects. You might have a new product out that you want some feedback on before the big launch. Why not ask some of these valued customers to help you, by having a preview of the new product ahead of the market?

You can ask them for help too sometimes, which may sound counterintuitive. For instance, if you've dealt with them for a while, you may want to ask for a reference that you can use on LinkedIn. This may seem odd, as you would think that ordinarily it should be you looking to help them rather than the other way around. But in fact, I find that people by their very nature like to help. Consequently, if you frame something in a way that suggests you're asking for their help, you may often be pleasantly surprised. Plus, it builds even more rapport.

Part of your LinkedIn invitation could look like this. You thank them for their business and then say something like, *"and I wonder if you'd be prepared to help me a little. I'm keen to update my LinkedIn profile and would like to ask if you could say a few kind (but truthful) words!"*

In the example of the new product being launched to market, your email could say something like this: *"...we have a new product, the XLT, that's about to be launched. At a meeting recently our sales manager asked if we knew of any companies that would be prepared to help us by trying out this product for a short period. I immediately thought of you. You have been a good customer of ours for a number of years, and you know how we operate and what we do. So, could I ask for your help please? Would you be prepared to take the new XLT and give it to your team to use for a couple of weeks? I will then drop you a form where you can give us some feedback. I hope you can help, please let me know in the next couple of days."*

This is also the group of people that you may want to offer upgrades to. Maybe your company has some premium products in stock that it cannot shift. This is an excellent opportunity to offer an upgrade to an existing loyal customer, or alternatively a new account that you want to break into. With your loyal customer you might be able to offer them some form of offer pricing just to encourage them to take the product. Just frame this in a way that reinforces the fact that this is a favour you're offering them. Depending on the product, and the amount of business they do with you, you might even offer them one for free. Particularly if you believe that they may come back and order a quantity of them subsequently. These are all the sorts of commercial decisions you need to make when you are in a sales role.

Be open

Alongside the qualities of honesty and integrity, it is also important to be open with your clients and prospects. Your communication style will therefore be light and friendly. Never make the customer feel wronged. If you do, they will simply avoid communicating with you. For instance, if they decide to place some business with one of your competitors, don't let any irritation show. Of course, you may have spent considerable time on putting together a proposal for them. They may have made you wait ages for their decision. But in any of these situations you need to accept their decision with good grace and move on. The game has just changed. If you've lost this order – it's gone, but what you're chasing now is the next one. This could be an order for a different product or service, or it may be the next time they are in the market for the one you just lost out on.

I think that it's always a good idea to try and find out the reason why somebody went elsewhere. The way I suggest framing this is that you are *"keen to learn"*, and that your company takes a positive view of feedback. Whatever the reasons, you want to learn for next time. This is a mature and grown up way of dealing with the situation and hopefully building the relationship for the long term. It may not reflect how you feel, but it is worth doing.

Anything you offer your customer, such as a proposal, is always good to set out in writing. Be an honest broker. Naturally, you might give them a price over the phone, but always follow up with a confirmation email. That way, there can never be any misunderstanding about what was said, or what is on offer.

Make dealing with you as transparent as possible. Your customers will like this and will respond to you better.

A quality that I think sits well with this is being calm. Whatever the situation, your customers will like it if you always seem calm and in control. Sometimes they may put extreme pressure on you to get things done for them. They might be in a mess and need helping out. Whether you're going to say yes or no, it always makes sense to do it in a professional, cool and calm manner. You always want to display that you're in control and know what's going on. Naturally, you would expect this of any doctor, surgeon or lawyer that you encountered. And that's because they're professionals. It seems a reasonable aspiration for any of us to have.

Do unto others...

Being a nice person is about treating people in the way that you like to be treated. That old biblical phrase, *"Do unto others as you would have them do unto you"* has a strong resonance here. Therefore, a great template for knowing how to behave with other people is to recognise and think about how you like to be treated when you are the customer. This seems like an excellent blueprint for the way that you should treat others. It probably needs a little bit of fine-tuning. Not everybody likes the same things as us, but nevertheless it's a good start point.

It's about your organisation's support too

The most difficult element in your relationship with your customer is around the support you have from your company or organisation. I say 'most difficult' because of course this is the one part you cannot necessarily control. But let us assume that you work for a good, professional company which wants to support you and your customers.

As a result of this, you will often be in a situation where you are caught in the middle of a negotiation. Clearly, you need to represent your company's interests and toe the party line when communicating with your customers. If you don't, your job is in jeopardy! Or more likely, you get overruled, which undermines your credibility with your customer. Nevertheless, you also need to play the role in reverse. You will often need to make representations on behalf of your customer to try and get them what you consider to be fair and reasonable treatment. Sometimes this means negotiating with your boss or other departments to get your customer the service they deserve. Sometimes, you need to tread a fine line. Your customer expects the best service they can get and will sometimes communicate this to you loudly. Potentially in contrast, your company needs to run a profitable business. You are in a frontline role though, and therefore it is part of your responsibility to represent the needs of your customers. Your company or organisation has a vested interest in listening to what you say. They may not go along with it on every occasion, but nevertheless they have a responsibility to listen. Therefore, make sure your communication is calm, considered, and professional.

As well as all this communication working effectively, your product or service needs to work well for them too. Ultimately that's what they are using.

Fortunately, my training has been well received over the years. So that aspect hasn't been a problem for me personally. In addition, I recognise that I control the whole relationship from start to finish, which makes things considerably easier.

Many of you will be in a situation where you are part of a distribution chain. Maybe you deal with a manufactured product. Maybe that comes from overseas. Maybe your factory has a shutdown for summer or periodic shutdowns for maintenance.

You may be powerless when a problem arises. However, a key part of your role as the salesperson is about liaising with your customer, always being available and finding the best way to smooth over the situation. It can be the ultimate test of the strength of the relationship you have worked so hard to build up.

People buy from people

This phrase is so true. As I said at the beginning of this chapter, they are buying you just as they are buying your company's products or services. In many instances the relationship they have with you may be more important than the product or service. How often do we hear of cases where a sales person leaves and takes many of their customers with them? This is because the loyalty to them personally is stronger than to the products or services they are buying.

Therefore, just as you want your company's products and services to be the best they can be, it's equally important that you try to be the best you can be.

I've talked about behaviour patterns in this chapter. Communication style is an equally important part of your relationship with your customer. Even your vocal tone has a significant part in painting a picture of what you're like as a human being. If you're in a frontline job making outbound calls and you never go to see your customers, then your voice and communication style is everything. They will even form a picture of what they think you look like. We have a bit of fun with this on training courses where we give some examples. Some of them come from me, but more come from the people I'm working with in the training environment.

When somebody is talking to you on the phone, subconsciously they start to think about your physical characteristics. This will include what colour hair you've got, how old you are, how tall you are, what style hair you've got, and what your body shape is! It also includes how attractive you are, so it's powerful stuff! The example I usually use with training teams if I think that they're not completely convinced is to pose a question to them. *"Who here has dealt with somebody on the phone for a period of time and then met them, only to discover that they look nothing like you imagined?!"* At this point nearly everybody smiles and starts nodding. Sometimes they give me some great stories. Often these will centre around their own colleagues: the salespeople out in the field. They will say something like *"I'd spoken to Sarah a few times but when I met her, she was nothing like I imagined. I thought she looked like ..."* and then all their colleagues laugh.

STORIES FROM THE FRONT

In one of the early telemarketing teams I managed in the forklift truck industry, one of the characters was larger than life. John was a good-looking lad, and he knew it. He spoke to a receptionist at a company in Maidenhead on two occasions and decided that he fancied her. Presumably, she felt the same way too, as they agreed to meet up for a date. John made the journey to see her, which was over 100 miles. And that was all based purely on how she sounded on the phone. From memory, it didn't go anywhere from there, so presumably they (or one of them) decided that the voice was actually better than the real person!

I did some training many years ago at a wholesale meat business. They had a team of three females making outbound calls. One of the ladies in the team, Sue, was a short, rotund middle-aged lady with short cropped red hair. As a wholesale business, they dealt with many accounts repeatedly. They were in effect account managers. Sue had a great personality and was what would commonly be described as bubbly. Sparky and friendly, with a great sense of humour. She told us that one of her regular customers had sent her lingerie in the post on more than one occasion. She thought that this was hugely funny and said, *"He would have a different view if he actually met me!"* I didn't know whether to laugh or be alarmed by this story. It certainly is a bit creepy, but again it shows the power of the human voice.

Be aware of the power of your voice. Your use of language, your vocal tone, your vocal pitch, and your enthusiasm, all come through to describe you in huge detail to the person on the other end of the line.

CHAPTER 4:
GET ORGANISED

In the previous chapter we considered the importance of you. Your role in building the relationship with the person on the other end of the line. The good news is that this is all completely within your control. Nevertheless, you need to be organised and work to a structured plan. If you have all the personality in the world, but no plan, it will feel like hard work. It's incredible how many field-based salespeople fit this description. I've worked with many over the years who have been excellent face-to-face with customers. However, in contrast, their administration was frequently extremely poor. Sales managers I have known and worked with frequently pull their hair out trying to ensure that basic company systems are adhered to. I guess it's all to do with skill sets. These two important elements of the job don't sit naturally within many people.

If you're developing sales as part of running your own business, then of course a lack of organisation will become an Achilles' heel for your business. If you recognise that this is the case for you, and you know that you are never likely to change, then it's worth employing some part-time or full-time help.

Prospecting, or business development work, is a process. It is important to recognise this and put in place whatever you can to fine-tune each element. Now, this is important: it doesn't just begin the moment you pick up the phone. Or at least it shouldn't do. Even if you're part of a telesales or telemarketing team, and you don't need to source your own leads, it is vital to be structured and organised.

You need a plan

A well-organised person will have a plan in place before the day even starts. If prospecting is part of that plan, and you are the owner of your own business or a sole trader, you should know today what tasks you want to action tomorrow. I use an American diary product called Day-Timer, which I've used for over 30 years. It's the equivalent of that famous 1980s' British icon - the Filofax. I use it to constantly jot down tasks or jobs that I need to do, days in advance. This system works for me, and it means that every day I already have a set of tasks that I have noted. Some may have been jotted down yesterday because I didn't complete them. Alternatively, they could be things that I wrote down a month ago. It wouldn't be relevant to go into too much more detail at this point. The point is that my own system works for me and has been refined over a period of years.

You need to find your own way of remembering, organising, and planning tasks in a way that works for you. This means finding a system which balances the time spent using it against the time saved by being well-organised. This may be fully electronic, fully paper-based, or a blend of the two. If you try to use a system which you find a chore, or complicated to use, or against your natural style of working, it will soon fall by the wayside.

Clearly, time management is extremely important in this area too. There are some brilliant books and courses on time management. However you go about it, it is worth trying to maximise your use of time.

I'll review the process of pre-call planning in detail in Chapter 8, including the specific things that you should do for each call. Any good plan starts with a bit of thinking in advance. Have an idea of who you plan to call in each spell of phoning and be clear about what you want to say. I have noticed that many of the most successful telemarketers or telesales people will generally get into the office 15 to 20 minutes early and spend this time getting organised. They may look at their database, review their day's contacts and remind themselves of notes they have made.

Prepare your list

In whichever way you organise yourself, I suggest that you should have your list ready in advance. If you are sat at your desk thinking about who you should phone next, the process will become disjointed and time will be wasted. You're more likely to become easily distracted and may drift away from the task. Something else will crop up that suddenly seems more important or more urgent. Also, by having a list, you can see clear progress being made during the day. I find that seeing the number of calls due or overdue decreasing is satisfying and motivating.

If you're working in a telesales or telemarketing team, the lack of a list is less likely to be an issue. You, or perhaps someone else, will have already produced the list of calls that you are due to make today. They know that having a system in place is necessary to get the best out of any team. In most B2B market sectors you will probably be able to make 100 calls in a day fairly comfortably. However, and obviously, you can only do this if you have a system and a structure.

That figure of 100 calls may surprise you. You might think that you will soon run out of people to call. Once you have phoned 100 or 1000 people, then what? The good news is that in B2B, it doesn't work like this. The size of the list you are likely to need to work with is in fact relatively small and manageable. In my prospect pot currently are around 1,200 names, and this size of database has sustained my business for over 20 years. Admittedly there are an additional 3,500 that I have archived. Nevertheless, let's round it up and call it 5,000 carefully selected names across 20 years. What happens is that you make 100 calls and on 75 of them, you don't get through to the person you need to speak to. So that's 75 of your 100 that you will then call again over the next few days. So, you won't need as many new names as you may first think. Nothing like. I should stress that I'm thinking specifically about B2B here. The numbers in B2C will be on a different scale.

On the calls where you get hold of people, there will be some where you will have a great conversation. You will enjoy these, and suddenly the job will feel rewarding. However, on the majority of first-contact calls, people won't want to engage in business with you immediately. But you've made a start, you've put the first small building-block in place in creating a relationship with that prospect.

There will be a variety of different outcomes which necessitate a future call. On one call you might have a great conversation with somebody that you've not previously spoken to. You talk to them about your products or services and you agree to send them some information, probably via email. Hopefully, you will have agreed to make a future contact to find out what they thought of your information. This could be a call in a couple of days' time or you might end up leaving it a month. Either way, it's always a good idea to agree the next call-back with the decision maker. If they have expressed interest, enough interest for you to send them something, this is a buying signal, so they are definitely worth following up.

Reasons or excuses?

On another call you might get a more lukewarm response. The person seems engaged and interested in your products or services, but it might be that they are not in the market for a set period of time. A common reason here might be a lack of budget. So the most significant thing they say might be something like, *"Yes, that could be of interest to us, but we're not going to be spending any money in that area until we get our new budget through in April."* You will check when they will start looking at this and agree to call them back at the appropriate time.

Another call outcome might be that the person you speak to is interested but they need to have a conversation with somebody else first. That could be their boss, or it could be someone in another department such as purchasing or marketing. Again, you will make an agreement to contact them back.

The reasons for callbacks will be numerous and varied, and so it is essential that you note them down in detail at the end of each call. You may call some businesses which are highly seasonal. If you catch them in peak season, they won't necessarily be interested in engaging with new suppliers. This is frequently the case for a business such as mine – training. They are hardly likely to look at training their customer service team if they are busy taking a huge number of calls at this time of year.

Then there are some factors relating to the person rather than the organisation. Your contact might tell you that they are leaving the company at the end of next month. In those circumstances, to make any headway with this company, it is better to hold off calling until the new person has got their feet under the desk.

Many companies you speak to will tell you that they are going through restructures, mergers, or buyouts. Something is happening within the organisational structure of the business which means that they're not looking at additional suppliers currently.

Then of course we all get the whole range of typical sales objections. Some people you speak to inevitably will be *"quite happy thank you"* dealing with one of your competitors. Or they are a company that has no money at this point.

In all the situations I've outlined above, you will want to keep in touch with them, and so this one contact on your list will necessitate a succession of future calls.

So, as I hope you can see, to make 100 outbound calls each day, you don't need anything like 100 new names every day. Thank goodness.

Prospecting as a process

Planning your activity clearly and methodically will yield huge dividends. So, think about everything in advance. Design it from start to finish. Each call should start with some pre-call planning.

During each call, it's vital to take notes while you're talking to decision makers. These just need to be the key facts. I simply use a pad that I've created out of scrap paper. You merely want to jot down some key facts and figures.

As soon as you have finished each call, enter your notes into whatever system you're using. Ideally, this should be some sort of CRM system. Or Excel at the very least. The quality of your notes here is crucial because they become the engine for your next call. The more relevant details you have that you can use to summarise back to the decision maker on your next call, the better. You can also use them selectively to get past gatekeepers. Your notes become your golden ticket back into that account.

When the receptionist asks, *"Have you spoken to Bob before?"* or *"What is the purpose of your call?"* or *"Is he expecting your call?"*, you have at your fingertips, in your notes, ways of proving that you've made previous contact. You can say something like, *"Yes, I spoke to Bob about six months ago, and we agreed to talk around now, following the company merger."* Or it might be, *"Yes, I've spoken to Sarah before. She asked me to recontact her after her holiday in Australia."* In both these instances you have given the receptionist enough evidence to reassure them that you have spoken to their colleague before. They are less likely to give you the brush-off.

If you're running your own business, or you're a field salesperson setting your own appointments, then the notes you use are hopefully your own. In this case, you have a vested interest in ensuring that the quality of your notes is as high as possible. However, there will be some instances when you're not using your own notes. For instance, if you are a new field salesperson working a sales patch that you've inherited from somebody else, you will start with their opinions, notes, and writing. There is not a lot you can do about this, particularly if the previous incumbent left poor or non-existent notes. You may need to ask your new boss for help in filling in some of the gaps. You can at least console yourself that every day you're working your new area, you will be improving the quality of information.

When making notes, the key start-point is to record details of dates, quantities, and locations. These are the basic facts needed to work out what type of sales opportunity you have. Keep your note-taking brief, as your key role when prospecting is to spend as much time as possible talking to customers. The administration must always play second fiddle. Don't waste time recording he-said, she-said type comments. Leave out the filler words and keep it brief. Even if you save a few seconds or minutes per note, over time this will add up. If your call pattern is to make just five prospecting calls each week, and you sell a complex technical product or service, in those circumstances lengthy notes may be worth the effort. But for most of us, keep them simple and brief. Over the years, I've also developed my own acronyms and abbreviations. These are great if it's your own business and only you read them, but they may need some explaining if other people are going to be working on your behalf.

Useful abbreviations

Here are some of mine! *Incidentally, I offer you these more for amusement than as a blueprint to use.*

Ooo	–	out of office
NA at mo	–	Not available at the moment
Nittat	–	not in today, try again tomorrow
Nitl	–	not in, try later
V-m, dlm	–	voicemail, didn't leave message
Lft msg v-m	–	*I'm sure you've got that one*

Of course, they need to be consistent. Otherwise you will look at your notes in 6 months' time and have no idea what the code means!

So, keeping it simple and brief works to your advantage. I recommend something such as

> *"Nim at mo (not in market at mo) as waiting for merger with ABC to go thro' summer. Also has new boss starting in May. Interested in our KLM range as used them when he worked at GHI."*

I think that the example above is as useful and easier to follow than this:

> *"Spoke to him at length. Seemed nice guy and open to new ideas. He said he's not sure what will happen*

regarding buying our product as it depends on how the new merger goes with ABC from France in summer at some point. He said he expects it to drag on until early autumn although it's supposed to be completed by July or August time. I agreed and said I know what he means. These deals usually take longer than anyone expects. He also said that Sarah his boss is going off on maternity leave in April, and so he will have a new boss from early May. He's not sure if this will be an internal appointment or an external one. He seemed really interested when I told him about our latest KLM range. He said that he knew of our products, as he used to use some of the KLM when he used to work at his previous employer GHI, based in Milton Keynes. Sounds like a good prospect for the future."

As you can see, the first, shorter, pithier example tells you all the key things you need to know. If you're making 30, 50 or 100 calls in a day, keeping your notes concise and to the point makes a big difference.

Reduce distractions

It's important to eliminate distractions as much as possible when you're making external calls. Otherwise, you tend to lose the rhythm. When you're calling, you will benefit from making a series of calls in quick succession. Avoid looking at emails while you're making outbound calls. It's a good idea to split your day up into hours. Make calls for an hour, and then peel off and check your emails, and maybe have a coffee. If you're organised and your system is working well, you can make 20+ calls during that hour. You probably won't achieve that hit-rate the first time you make calls in that way but, supported by a good system, you soon will.

Activity on the phone generates activity off the phone. This is a good thing because this is what you are trying to achieve. You are trying to put energy and activity out there, and what you want is to stimulate activity coming back. For example, you may need to send emails to the people who have expressed interest in having more information.

Use templates

With any of this supporting activity, I strongly recommend using templates. I do love a good template!

The beauty of using templates to send out information is that it significantly reduces the amount of time you spend writing. You simply copy and paste into your email, and maybe top and tail it. Just add a specific tailored opening, and maybe the same at the end. The bulk of each email can be largely the same. Just take some time and care in drafting the core text that you are going to use across multiple emails. And ensure that there are no spelling mistakes by reviewing it carefully.

It is likely that you will need a comprehensive series of templates. You may need an introductory one for people interested in one of your product divisions. You might have a separate letter if you're sending something to organisations in the public sector. The list goes on. Build up your archive of templates as each new application arises. If you're working in a telemarketing or telesales team, ask your boss or support team to provide you with a good selection of templates to cover most eventualities.

Writing a perfectly crafted piece of prose may take you 20 minutes, but when you have produced it, it can be used afresh multiple times.

Using a CRM system

Knowledge is power when it comes to making phone calls, and if you're in a customer service role dealing with incoming calls. So, it is important to have all the information that you may need easily accessible in one place. Back in the old days, by which I mean the mid-'80s, this meant relying on a paper-based system. We had two great administrators who supported our telemarketing team. Maxine and Kay made sure that everybody had all their calls on individual record cards every day. When I look back at that now, it seems incredible. The idea of constantly filing and updating record cards to keep this team of six telemarketers busy every day, each making over 100 calls, is amazing. But that's how we all had to work back then. There was no alternative, and of course it's what we were used to. Of course, we now have computers to help us. They are designed perfectly for this function. The data we need will be plentiful, easy to access and is likely to be in a consistent format.

It is likely that you will have access to some form of customer relationship management (CRM) system. These CRM systems are specifically designed to help you manage your outbound call pot. There are two separate approaches to this. If you are employed as an office-based telemarketing or telesales executive, you will almost certainly work using the company's CRM system. You won't have any say in this; you will join and be shown how to use the system. It's the same if you're in field-based sales and you want to access information about your regular customers and other prospects on your patch.

Choosing a CRM system

However, if you are phoning on behalf of your own business or you are just starting out, you have a wealth of choice. I'm not here to advise you on which CRM system to select. Technology changes so rapidly that the best advice today may well be out of date within a year or so. If you're choosing a CRM system for your own business, I suggest you spend a bit of time looking around. This is an important investment for you, as a good system will optimise your working processes. If you're self-employed, or running a small business, my advice would be to start out with a relatively straightforward system. You don't need to invest large sums in an all-singing, all-dancing corporate system. Do your own research. It's also a good idea to get some personal recommendations. Ask other people what system they use and what they think about it. However, choose friends or connections working in a similar sized business to yours to receive relevant recommendations.

The issue of cost shouldn't prevent you from choosing a suitable CRM system. The time it saves will repay you many times over. Another approach to consider, which will cost nothing in terms of finance, and will at least get you going, is to use Microsoft Excel. If your business is only you, and you make a relatively low number of calls, then Excel will probably do the job, if set up properly. You can manage most aspects of your call pot in Excel, but it becomes clunky if you want to start being more sophisticated in your approach, such as selecting and filtering for email campaigns. For any business with two or more people accessing the organisation's sales and marketing data, the argument for investing in a proper CRM system wins the day.

Any system needs to be designed around the fact that you talk to human beings. On your front screen you need the name of the company, its address including postcode, plus a field or fields with details of the decision-makers or influencers in the business. This should include space for email addresses and mobile numbers too.

With all this data, it is vitally important to make sure that it is 100% accurate. Or at least as close to that as you can possibly get. If you have a general tendency to be pedantic in life, then you are a great person to manage the data inputs in a CRM.

STORIES FROM THE FRONT

At one company I worked at, I inherited a member of staff, Jenny, a South African. I built the CRM system for our business, which had six separate trading divisions. Jenny was a very competent administrator, and I gave her the job of overseeing the quality of data in our new system. She really came into her own and proved to be brilliant at this part of the role. She had really high standards around what went into our system. However, she often communicated this in a rather harsh and brusque way with the telephone team. Nevertheless, ultimately this all worked out well. The members of the phone team respected her abilities and knew that they couldn't get away with anything. And on the other hand, it was my job to ensure that she wasn't too hard on them individually.

Accuracy is key

All the details in this part of the system need to be accurate, for a variety of reasons. Clearly, the easiest way of offending somebody is to get their name wrong. You need to ensure that the spelling is correct. If customers are reeling off phone numbers of colleagues or other company sites, again telephone numbers are completely useless unless they're 100% accurate. The same goes with email addresses too. So, it's worth having some high standards around this subject. Clearly, any email campaigns you run as a business will be powered by the data in your CRM system. And if you send marketing letters in the post, they should be generated from the addresses you have in your CRM system. You need to ensure that your one system of contact with your customer base can be used effectively to power the rest of your marketing.

What do you do if you inherit a customer database which you know is out of date, or extremely poor quality? The answer to this depends on how poor it is. The advice from many consultants would generally be to simply bin it and start again. However, there are other options, before you rush to take this nuclear option.

There are brokerages who will clean your data. If you're going to use this service, I would advise you to work with a big well-known reputable company.

You send these agencies your poor-quality database, and they then run it past their huge database. For a fee, they will add the missing parts (called appending) you need to your data. Another option could be to employ someone such as a student to work on it as a project and to undertake some desk-based research. This may include looking up companies on the internet to check if they still exist. Often it also involves making calls to check that the phone still gets answered, and that the decision makers listed on your system still work at the company. This exercise doesn't need to cost much money but will make outbound calling so much more effective. There's a psychological benefit to this too. If you or your employees spend time on the phone contacting dead companies and poor data, they will soon lose motivation. So, it cannot be overstated: quality of data is king. The often-quoted comparison between the scatter gun approach and laser guided missiles springs to mind.

STORIES FROM THE FRONT

In the early days of running outbound telemarketing teams in the forklift truck industry, I was summoned to go and see the marketing director one day. This was a slightly strange occurrence, as I seldom had any individual dealings with my boss's boss. My own boss, Tony, was very hands-on and most of what I ever did went through him. The marketing director to me seemed rather aloof. He wasn't a scary person; in fact, he was all charm and personality. Nevertheless, he worked at a different office to me, over 100 miles away, and so I rarely spoke to him directly. However, I wasn't particularly concerned as I went off to his office.

We had recently run a mail campaign to a large, carefully filtered selection of our database. The reason he'd summoned me soon became evident as he passed me one of the letters that our direct mail team had sent out. The customer had very kindly returned it to us.

The members of our phone team are human beings of course. And there are some people they speak to on the phone who they don't particularly warm to. Therefore, some of them would sometimes make notes to themselves about somebody who was particularly unpleasant, so that they were ready on the next call. I'm sure these types of transgressions would be less likely to happen these days. Of course, it may be fine to put these comments or your own feelings in any of the fields in your CRM system. However, for the dear love of whoever you pray to, as will become clear, don't put these comments in the job title field.

James T, one of the members of our phone team, had written in the job title field 'Miserable bastard.' I can't remember if that was exactly what he put, as it was a long time ago. But that was certainly the gist of it. The poor customer receives a letter in the post with his name in the top left corner, and the words 'Miserable bastard' underneath. As soon as John, our marketing director, showed me the letter, I of course felt incredibly embarrassed. In fairness to him, he didn't give me a hard time, and nor did he really reprimand me. However, he didn't need to because I completely understood the gravity of the situation. This short meeting was followed quickly by me talking to the whole team and showing them what had happened. To the best of my memory, it never happened again. Thank goodness! I can look back now and afford myself a chuckle...

The importance of postcodes

Another part of a company's address details which is crucial to get right is the postcode. Especially if you send out direct mail. Probably more significant though is that within many corporate organisations, sales territories are determined by postcode. So, it's important when talking to the customer on the phone to ensure you get the correct one. This may have an impact on which of your sales colleagues you send to see them. It may also have an impact on which territory any sale is allocated to. In either of these circumstances, inaccuracies and errors can lead to loud complaints. Logistics and transport also work off postcodes. So, treat them with great respect. You could potentially have the wrong distribution hub trying to deliver items if the postcode on your system has been wrongly input. When taking down details of a postcode, always check it back with the customer. As we all know over the phone, 'M' sounds like 'N', 'B' sounds like 'P', and 'S' sounds like 'F'. It can be good practice to use the phonetic alphabet to repeat letters back ie A for Alpha, B for Bravo etc. If your geographical knowledge of the UK is poor, be extra careful. A delivery going to an ME postcode is quite different to an NE postcode, and yet on the phone they may sound similar. And a PO postcode exists, but a BO one doesn't.

It's also important to record details of contact history. You need to know facts such as when they were last contacted and what was said. This contact history may go back years. Consequently, it's important that all contact history is in reverse chronological order. The most recent conversation is the part you will most likely need to read over. Conversations that happened five years ago will almost certainly not be useful.

As for the rest of it, it largely depends on whether it's your own managed database or you are working your company's one. For a strongly divisionalised company, it may be useful to have some sort of flags to denote which of your divisions this customer may be relevant to.

If you have some historic sales data in your system, then of course this will help you when making calls. You need to make the call as tailored to the person you speak to as possible. Knowing what products or services they bought from you in the past, and when, and the quantities ordered, will all be useful things to draw on to mould your conversation.

It may be useful to have some information which denotes the industry type relating to each customer. This is useful marketing data, as it allows you to send targeted communication to them. Historically, this was based around universal SIC codes. However, this system is crude, as it is so generic. Why not create your own coding system to fit your own company's needs? However, keep it simple and easy to understand by making the industry codings as brief and specific as possible. If they are too complicated and the employee filling out the record can't quickly identify the correct code, they will guess or leave the field blank, if they can, which renders the system useless.

You probably don't need much else in your CRM system. It just needs to reflect what you and your company regards as important customer information. Over the years, I've seen some obscure data dutifully entered which I suspect never gets used. The irony is that the more data you attempt to get people to complete, the less they will. If it all takes too long and feels a purely bureaucratic exercise, the data will rapidly become out of date and incomplete.

Monitoring activity

If you're in a telesales or telemarketing role your call activity will almost certainly be recorded. And I don't mean in the form of call recording where the company stores the full transcript of some, or all, your calls.

I'm talking here about the idea of recording some basic data so that you know how effective your outbound calling is. If you manage an outbound team, you should have some data recording in place. If you're self-employed, or making calls for your own business, you may feel that you don't need this extra layer of bureaucracy or administration. There is only you, and you are only accountable to yourself.

However, I regard it as useful and necessary to gather statistics about the effectiveness of your call activity. In fact, I would say, from my own experience, that it makes the task more fulfilling, as you gain a measurable sense of progress. Why wouldn't you want to know how effective this form of marketing is in your own business?

Even though I work as a freelance self-employed trainer, I use the same system to count activity as I did when I first started the business over 20 years ago. This proven system is also the one I used with the teams I managed when I was employed. I'm so clear on its benefits that I also sell it as a system to companies I work with.

It's easy to administer and is based around recording four key statistics. These four stats are all you need to know about each member of your team, or about your own activity personally. Incidentally, the system I'm about to describe doesn't generally get covered by CRM systems. Within your CRM system you are inputting data. So, it's all about quality. With *To Market's* telemetrics system that I'm about to outline it's merely about activity. Just raw data. There are some quality measures built-in, but I'll explain that in what follows.

Dials per hour

At the end of each call, I put a little tick in a box. The activity sheets are pre-printed, so I simply have one at my side when I'm on the phone. For each hour then, I know how many outbound calls I've made. Dials per hour simply gives me a measure of activity. There's nothing about results. There's nothing about effectiveness, but it does tell you how hard you are working. If you're managing a team of callers, it also allows you to start making comparisons between their relative performance. For instance, if you have got one member of your team who averages 14 calls per hour, all other things being equal they will probably be twice as successful as somebody averaging 7 calls an hour.

Contacts per Hour (or DMPs)

The next number to measure is how many times you get through to the right contact. So, you refer to this as Contacts per Hour, or Decision-Maker Presentations (DMPs.) Unless you're highly skilled, or just lucky, this number will probably seem quite low compared with your dials per hour. It's important to log the number of decision makers you get through to. This is because these are your real sales opportunities. This is when selling can begin. This is when you start to flex your sales muscles. It doesn't matter how good you are at selling, if the person you want to speak to isn't there, or is on holiday, or is in a meeting, you don't have an opportunity to achieve your desired outcome. Therefore, it's important to know how many genuine opportunities you have.

It's difficult for me to give you an accurate guide because it depends on your industry sector and the type of calls you are making. Nevertheless, to give you an example, you might find that making 10 to 15 calls in an hour might only result in one or two DMPs. The rest of the time, you simply will not get through to the person you need to speak to, for a variety of reasons.

What does this figure tell you? Firstly, it's used in the calculation of conversion rate, which is in the next section. It also tells you something about the skill and tenacity of your phone behaviour. Often, members of a team who have a comparatively high level of DMPs will be clever in how they manage to get hold of the decision maker. For instance, they might be effective at befriending receptionists and PAs. They might be creative and try contacting this person at either end of the office day. They might send them an email saying that they will call them at a particular time, and what the call is about. Being creative in the way that you approach decision-makers can only help you get through to more of them.

Conversion rate

Ok, now for a bit of maths. The whole reason for making all these calls is to try and generate a particular result. We'll refer to this as the desired outcome. If you're working in a telemarketing team setting appointments for your field-based colleagues, then your desired outcome is to secure an appointment. Complete with a time and date in the diary. If you're in a telesales role, then your desired outcome is to achieve a sale. We're not interested at this point in the value of it or the number of items ordered. It's merely about managing to get a sale out of this customer.

Now we look at the number of appointments or sales orders you achieve as a percentage of the number of Contacts per Hour or DMPs you get through to. This is your true sales effectiveness. In the previous section I talked about recording the number of DMPs you have achieved. Let's say, over the course of 2 weeks someone in your team manages to get through to 100 decision-makers. From these, one of your team members, Kieron, has managed to achieve 8 sales. This therefore is a conversion rate of 8%. Eight out of the 100. The person sat next to Kieran, James, has spoken to 80 decision makers and achieved 4 sales over the same period. Consequently, James conversion rate is 5%. (4/80)

If you're managing a team, being able to make clear comparisons between your team members is essential in gauging how to manage and motivate each member of your team.

Output per hour

The fourth and final measurement is output per hour. If you're running a telemarketing team, then this will probably be appointments per hour. If it is a sales team then it may well be the number of sales made in each hour as an average. This is the number of times that each member of the team generates the desired outcome for each hour that they spend on the phone. To a large degree this fourth measure is a function of the previous three statistics.

For instance, if somebody racks up a high number of dials per hour, and they get through to a good number of people, and they achieve a high conversion rate, then their output per hour will be high. The same works in reverse. If they don't conduct much activity on the phone, and they're not effective at getting hold of people, and then when they do, they don't convert many, they will inevitably have a very low output per hour rate.

Of the four measures detailed here, this is the one that most managers will focus on. Especially if you're the boss paying them. Everybody wants to see a return on their investment. Consequently, the statistic most directors, company owners, or bosses will be interested in is for each hour that I pay them to sit at their desk, what do they produce?

Relating this measure per hour allows for meaningful comparisons between team members. For example, you can easily compare your part-time members of staff with your full-time members. Similarly, if there are more disruptions during one specific week or day, and people are pulled away into meetings or briefings, then your monitoring system will take account of this. You will only be measuring the desired output from the actual time that somebody is on the phone. This should be measured in blocks of 15 minutes. Don't get too carried away by trying to record it to the minute.

Not only will you be able to compare results between individual team members, but you can also do this over time. How is each person performing compared with the same time last week, last month or last year?

You can also make comparisons between the results of various campaigns. As you might expect, these may vary wildly.

If it's your own business, why wouldn't you want to know how this ratio is working for you? Ultimately you want to know what you generate from the time you spend on the phone. Input and output, that is the ultimate arbiter. Add to that an understanding of *how* those results were achieved. Then, if you expand and decide to employ someone to conduct the calling for you, you can set realistic expectations, as you now understand the dynamics.

By recording these four measures, and understanding what each of them tells you, you can understand each phoner's results profile. It's not just about the ultimate outcome, but it's also about how they achieve them.

Let's consider this table of results

Name	Dials per hour	DMPs per hour	Conversion rate	Appts/Sales per hour
Susan	8.2	1.8	3%	0.06
Phil	15.0	2.5	7%	0.17
Vicki	14.7	3.3	8%	0.27
Jack	12.9	2.0	6%	0.13

Once you start to look at results comparatively, you can start to see patterns emerge. Simply saying, *"Work harder"* to try to improve results is a blunt and crude message which is unlikely to achieve improvements and certainly won't motivate your team. One size does not fit all when it comes to managing a phone team.

The beauty of the telesales function is that all activity is quantifiable. So, your management can be objective, scientific, based on data and measurement, rather than subjective and focused on personalities. It allows you to treat each member of the team individually, using detailed analysis of their areas of strength and weakness. Remember the old management adage

"You can't manage what you don't measure."

As the table shows, you have some work to do with Susan. But this can be discussed using indisputable facts. You can draw a cause–and–effect line between the dials per hour and the ultimate achievement of appointments/sales per hour. You can show clear evidence of how her colleagues have achieved more by improving the start-point of dials per hour. Susan now has a clear focus of where to improve rather than just being told to work harder.

Summary

Developing a system and seeing outbound calling as a scientific process will help you to get the most from each stage of activity. It's important that any system is designed to support you and help you to get the most out of the function. Don't let it become merely a bureaucratic requirement where you end up with the 'tail wagging the dog.' Keep it simple, and make sure it only gives you the data, the facts, and the trends you need to improve how you, or your teams, work.

CHAPTER 5:

WHY QUESTIONS ARE THE ANSWER

Questioning and listening are the two most important communication skills that you need when talking to customers. Therefore, it's worth honing your skills in these two areas. If you have good communication skills in general, then clearly everything else you try to achieve will become much easier.

The good news is that we are all naturally born to be inquisitive. If you have children and think back to a time when they were young, you will know what I mean! Small children ask questions naturally and persistently. After all, it's their way of learning. How can they increase their knowledge about the world around them without asking questions? Over time, as we get older, we are taught to drop this habit. Parents will say things such as, *"Stop being so nosey"* or, *"Stop asking so many questions"* or, when stumped for an answer, *"I don't know, that's just the way it is."* So, by the time we become adults, much of our natural inquisitiveness has been conditioned out of us.

However, when you're dealing with customers, it's important to reconnect with your natural inquisitiveness, your latent ability to ask questions. Keep asking questions and make them as incisive as possible. This is regardless of whether you are making calls or receiving them. If this was a book about customer service, I would be stressing the importance of questioning in exactly the same way.

The two key types of question

Our focus here is on two types of question: open and closed.

Let's start by considering the definition of a closed question. These are questions that require a 'yes' or 'no' answer. You may be able to think of a few exceptions to this, so I find it useful to use the following definition:

A closed question is **"a question that receives an answer of yes or no – or is intended to."**

In other words, the person asking the question is anticipating that you will give them a straight 'yes' or 'no'. Some examples of closed questions include the following

"Is that your coat on the back of the chair?"

"Have you bought from us before?"

"Did you say your budgetary year starts in April?"

If those are closed questions, now let's consider what possibilities an open question creates for you.

The benefits of open questions

If you ask a question and the answer cannot be 'yes' or 'no', then you are encouraging the person to give you more information. That is the first significant benefit of open questions. You're encouraging them to talk.

The second benefit, which leads on from this, is that open questions encourage them to open up and provide more information. The third benefit is that the conversation will feel more involving for them. Your aim is to make every customer interaction feel as much like a natural conversation as possible. Therefore, the more involved they feel, the more likely they are to enjoy their communication with you.

The main thing that most people like talking about is themselves. So, by asking open questions you allow them to do precisely that. As they do this, chances are they will tell you things that you want and need to know. This makes your job considerably easier. The very fact that you encourage them to talk also displays interest in them and their business. They are likely to respond positively to this. Where does all this loveliness lead to? Well, it helps you build a better two-way relationship with them, especially if they are asking questions of you as well. This builds rapport.

There are two key communication skills needed in building rapport. Listening is one, and asking open questions is the other. If you are naturally inquisitive and ask plenty of open questions, and you also listen carefully to the responses you get from the other person, you will almost certainly find it very easy to build rapport with people. Conversely, if you're not the slightest bit interested in other people, don't ask them questions, and don't listen to their responses, then you will find it very difficult to build rapport.

Open questions are therefore enormously powerful. Furthermore, they are easy to remember because you only need 7 words from the English language. The 7 open question words are:

* Who
* What
* When
* Where
* How
* Why
* Which

They are easy to remember because they have so much in common. They are sometimes collectively known as the 'W' words. Having written them up on the flip chart, on one course many years ago, I did ask the group in front of me why they are easy to remember. One delegate on this course, Duncan, was the MD and founder of a construction supplies company. He answered the question by saying, *"They've all got an H in them."* And of course, he is right. But that's not the easy way of remembering them. I used to get on well with Duncan and he had a very disarming sense of humour. He also had the ability to throw verbal curveballs from time to time which made him difficult to read on occasion. I often ask delegates on a course, before I start, whether they refer to the people they deal with as customers or clients. I asked this of a couple of members of Duncan's company. Quick as a flash one of the internal sales ladies said, *"Duncan won't let us call them clients. He says prostitutes have clients – we have customers!"*

The power of closed questions

Now, we have defined closed questions. Using that word 'closed' may imply that they are only of limited value. I sometimes meet people who have been trained previously that open questions are good and closed questions are bad. However, this isn't true at all. Both open and closed are extremely useful; you just need to know when to use each type. Getting a straight 'yes' or 'no' out of somebody can be exactly what you want on many occasions. Let's consider some of the benefits of using closed questions.

First, they are useful in helping you to obtain specific information. *"Have you dealt with our company before?"* You will probably take the conversation in a different direction depending on how they answer this question. *"And did the company merger go through a couple of months ago?"* These are all the types of questions you could ask somebody either over the phone or face-to-face that will help you to steer the call in the direction you need.

They are also useful when seeking clarification. This can be to clarify things in your own mind, or to help your customer gain clarification on some information. *"OK, so you prefer the 760 ZXT because, although it's more expensive, it is a much faster machine, is that right?"* In that instance, you would clarify something you need to know. To help them understand things, you might say something like, *"OK, I'll go away and look into that, and I'll put together a proposal for you. I'll send it through to you next Tuesday. Is that OK?"* You will find that you use closed questions naturally without necessarily thinking about them consciously. But they are excellent in these types of situation.

They are also useful when trying to gain some form of commitment from the customer. Often, salespeople will tell me that they use closed questions to close the deal. And yes, of course, this is absolutely right. However, I prefer the word 'commitment' to 'close'. That is because securing an order from a customer may often involve a number of different commitment stages. These don't all necessarily win you the order, but they do help you to edge closer to it. It's important to remember that although your ultimate aim is to obtain a commitment to an order or to generate an appointment, there are many other things you can do that will help you along the way. Consider some of the following:

> *"OK, great, could I bring along our product next week to run through a demonstration for you?"*

> *"What I'll do then is send you a login so that you can trial our service for the next 7 days. Does that sound OK?"*

> *"I'll send you an email about our products and services, and I'll include a link to our website. I'll then give you a call next week when you've had a chance to read it. Is that alright?"*

In each case, a 'yes' from your prospect/customer is taking you one stage nearer to securing an order.

In the chapter about structuring the sales call I will provide more details about the different forms of commitment that you can ask for.

Sometimes you use closed questions simply to secure some form of confirmation or affirmation from a customer. You might say something like, *"It might take me a while to look into this for you, but I'll give you a call before the end of the week just to update you. Is that alright?"*

Closed questions can also speed up the process of communication. The more you can focus on specifics the quicker you are likely to get the job done. However, if you use them in the wrong place, you are in danger of making the conversation feel too blunt and transactional. It won't give the customer that warm fuzzy feeling.

Use closed questions to round off a conversation as you're wrapping it up, and to focus the customer's choices on your preferred options. *"OK, so of the alternatives we have talked about, you're most interested in the 760 ZXT. Is that right?"* You will sometimes need closed questions to deal with somebody who tends to waffle or ramble. Your closed questions will help them to stay focused on your key points.

Some commonly used words that form closed questions are:

Do	Is	Will	Have	Could
Does	Are	Can	Has	Would
Did	Shall	May	Had	Should

So that's open and closed questions. Hopefully, the distinction between them is clear. However, I'm now going to muddy the waters by introducing camouflage questions.

Camouflage questions

These are questions which are always, always, always open. They are never closed. They are open for two reasons. First, the answer cannot be 'yes' or 'no', and secondly they must contain one of the seven 'W's. However, you use them for the same reasons as you would closed questions. So, although they are technically open, they are not great arm-round-the-shoulder rapport building questions. Hence that's why I call them camouflage questions. They are one thing but look like something else. This is most easily explained by giving you an example. A camouflage type of open question might be:

"When do you want delivery?"

Or possibly

"How many do you have in stock at the moment?"

These are both clearly open questions based on the definition we considered earlier. However, in both instances you are seeking specific information. So, you're using them for the same reasons as you would a closed question. Camouflage questions don't have any specific role in structuring your communication. It's just useful to be aware that open questions effectively sit on a scale. And these ones are right at the bottom of the scale near the borderline with closed questions. So, what questions sit at the other end of the scale? What type of questions are the most open ones that you can possibly ask?

Anything that asks people about their thoughts, feelings and opinions are likely to be the most expansive type of questions you can ask. Clearly, they need to be set in context. But nevertheless, generally people have thoughts, feelings and opinions about most things. And they love sharing them! So, if you're trying to build rapport with a new customer or you are trying to get somebody to chat, these are great questions to ask.

"How was your holiday to the States then?"

"What do you think trading will be like over the next year or so for your business?"

"And how did that make you feel?"

You do need to be careful with the question around feelings. It largely depends on how well you know the other person, and what you are talking about. It's also interesting to note, that generally us men feel less comfortable asking these questions than you ladies do. So always go with what feels natural.

The structure of your sales call

There is a great maxim to remember around questioning techniques.

"Remember to use open questions to open your call and use closed questions to close it."

Imagine your conversation as being a bit like the funnel pictured overleaf.

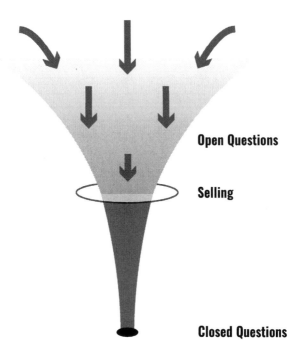

Open Questions

Selling

Closed Questions

The arrows going into the top of the funnel represent pieces of information. So, early on in your call, you'll ask all sorts of open questions that will help you navigate your way through the conversation.

"Who do you buy from at the moment?"

"What do you think of the suppliers you're with currently?"

"How many do you generally buy at a time?"

"When is the restructure due to happen?"

Once you've obtained some key nuggets of information from the customer, this then allows you to start telling them what you and your organisation provides. Doing it this way round at least gives you the chance of making sure that what you tell the customer is relevant to their needs. So that's when you do the selling, part way into the conversation. Not right at the beginning. Remember, they want to talk about them.

And then, as the conversation draws to a close, you use your closed questions so that you can finish the call at a defined endpoint.

> *"I'll send you the proposal in the next two days and I'll then give you a call early next week. Is that OK?"*

> *"I'll look into that, and I will give you a call back by tomorrow morning, alright?"*

> *"Do you have any further questions?"*

Towards the end of a conversation, you need to reach an agreement with somebody. Use your closed questions so that you're both clear on what happens next.

When I first heard about this maxim it was in relation to selling. However, I quickly realised that it works equally well in reactive customer service situations too.

WORDS OF WISDOM

The function of genius is not to give new answers but pose new questions which time and mediocrity can resolve.

Prof. Hugh Trevor-Roper

The TED principle

The TED principle is a useful tool to help you soften your questioning. Sometimes, you may try to gain a large amount of information but feel uncomfortable with this slightly intrusive or interrogative approach. You can soften this by mixing up your questions within other topics of conversation and some general chat. Avoid asking a series of questions in rapid succession. To soften the front end of some of your questions, use these elements of TED. You will find that they make your questioning sound softer. Use any of the following three options at the beginning of your question. TED stands for:

- Tell me
- Explain
- Describe

Consider these examples:

"Tell me, how do you usually decide who to buy these products from?"

"Explain what's important to you when you're choosing a new supplier for your PPE."

"Describe what it is you feel your boss is looking for with this contract."

Summary

In this chapter, we've considered the following three elements of questioning techniques:

* Open, closed and camouflage questions
* How to know when to use each type
* How to structure a good business conversation around effective questioning techniques

This is based around the use of **OPEN** & **CLOSED** questions. Good questioning skills are fundamental to many jobs, to obtain the correct information quickly and to identify where you can take the conversation. On the phone, whether you are selling, appointment setting, working on a technical help desk or dealing with customer queries and complaints, developing good questioning skills will pay huge dividends.

CHAPTER 6:

SAYING YES TO NOS: HANDLING COMPLAINTS, OBJECTIONS AND NOS

"One man's problem is another man's opportunity"

Dealing with any form of negative communication, whether it is a complaint, objection, or someone simply saying 'No' to you, is usually the most uncomfortable aspect of communication. Especially when you're dealing with people you don't know. This is because you have no history with them. Consequently, you don't know how to put ideas across in a way that will resonate with them. You have no relationship to draw on, and you have no credits in the bank. It is difficult to win them round.

It's worth bearing in mind though that every new customer or client relationship starts with some sort of initial conversation. Clearly, if we only ever dealt with people we've previously spoken to, business would eventually dry up and heal over.

For many people, that opening conversation is one of the most common reasons why people who don't sell say they wouldn't want to.

It is an overwhelming fear of rejection. Even in a situation where you have no reason to believe that the person on the other end of the phone will be antagonistic towards you, it is natural to worry about that opening reaction being one of, *"I'm not interested."* The stakes are then so much higher when the call involves handling a complaint or an objection to your sales pitch. Our natural tendency is to take these criticisms personally. It's not so much that they don't like our company or its products, but much, much worse than that, we fear that THEY DON'T LIKE US!

When we're in this frame of mind it becomes difficult of course to focus on what is being said. The emotions of rejection get in the way of the comments about our products and services. At this point, all too often, many of our natural communication skills desert us, just when we need them most. We stop listening so carefully and are less likely to make notes. We're more likely to lose our ability to direct the conversation, and our natural tone of voice deserts us. Inwardly, we're more likely to panic, to the point where the customer is aware of this and forces us even further on the defensive. Clearly this is likely to have an impact on how we deal with the customer or prospect's communication.

These emotions and fears never leave us, but successful salespeople become better at dealing with them. It's not natural, but we can build up resilience, develop a tougher shell and find ways to think more clearly even when under pressure.

Overcoming barriers

A more positive way of looking at any form of complaint, objection or 'no' is simply as a barrier to be overcome. It is important to remember that a customer who is taking the time to complain is at least presenting you with an opportunity. They are telling you about something that they want you to resolve. Ironically, this is preferable to the customer who never tells you and simply walks away. At least you can do something about it. You are still 'in the game'.

When training teams, I often use a customer service example. Say, historically, you have a one-in-three success rate in turning disgruntled customers into happy bunnies. They start off confronting you with *"I want to complain about this"* and by the end of the call, they are thanking you for your time and indicating that they are looking forward to trading with you again. What a satisfying outcome!

That one-in-three rate is far better than you can ever achieve if they are unhappy but *don't* complain, where you have zero chance of fixing things because you never get to hear about it, however skilled, knowledgeable, and passionate you are. Successfully handling complaints and sales objections is often the most satisfying phone interactions you can have. These are the ones you work hard to 'win.' You will never please all the people all of the time, but you can improve customer retention rates with some skilful communication around the more thorny issues!

However, our natural inclination is to try and avoid any form of negative communication. Complaints, objections, and 'No's become things to be feared, or guarded against. Or preferably avoided altogether. Most of us naturally wouldn't willingly go into a situation where we feel we will be given a hard time. Instead, our natural inclination is to either defend ourselves, or attack, or change, or ignore the ideas we are receiving. And of course, whilst this is happening it makes good 2-way conversation much less likely.

The key is to **adopt a different mental attitude.** This is of course easier to say than to do. However, here is a useful thought: *"You can't change what has happened to you, but you can change how you respond to it."* Adjust your mindset to deal with the situation objectively rather than subjectively. This will make a huge difference to the success you are likely to have in dealing with any form of negative communication.

Objective vs. Subjective

Let's look at the Oxford dictionary definition of objectivity:

"the object of perception or thought as distinct from perceiving or thinking subjectively." It says, *"external to the mind, real"* and then most significantly it says, *"being objective is dealing with outward things and not with thoughts or feelings – exhibiting actual facts uncoloured by the exhibitor's feelings or opinions."*

And the definition of subjectivity:

"taking place within the thinking subject, having its source in the mind, being personal, individual, introspective" and even goes on to talk about it being *"imaginary or illusory."*

So, to deal with a situation objectively means you stick to the facts of the case, no more, no less. If you deal with the situation subjectively, you are thinking about how it makes you *feel*. You are thinking more about your feelings than you are about the situation that is causing them. The danger of dealing with a situation subjectively is that you allow your emotions to dictate how you react. This will frequently cause problems. You need to leave emotion out of the situation as much as you possibly can. This may not be easy, but it is important.

A seven-step process

Given our natural tendency towards subjectivity, you need to take the following steps to stay in control:

1. **Pay attention**, by duplicating fully. By this I mean repeat back the key things to the other person. It works for you, and it works for them. Firstly, it clarifies your understanding. You need to ensure that you have understood the other person's viewpoint before you start to respond. This is what this does for you. Secondly, it works for them too. It reassures them. It demonstrates that you are listening, and taking it, and therefore them, seriously. The third benefit is that while you are repeating back the key things, it buys you some valuable time. Time to think. Thinking about what you're going to say next. How you are going to respond. The very fact that you're taking time to repeat information to them helps both of you to bring the situation into perspective.

2. **Make no assumptions.** When hearing negative communication, it is easy to blow it out of proportion. Even if it's a full complaint, don't assume that they never want to deal with you again. Even if they don't want to buy from you today, it doesn't mean they won't tomorrow, or the next day.

3. **Acknowledge their comments**, by repeating the essence fully. A partial or insincere acknowledgement will often just make the situation worse. If they say, *"Yeah, well, we're quite happy buying from ABC down the road"*, to simply respond by saying, *"Our products are really good, and we sell loads of them"* doesn't

really make the customer feel listened to. It would be more effective to ask them what they buy from ABC, or why they like them.

4. **Get involved in the conversation.** Natural communication is a 2-way process. It will feel better for both parties if it is like this. Therefore, be prepared to give some input. Provide information and explanations. Always aim to engage them in conversation.

5. **Ask questions.** This is a key part of directing a conversation. You can nudge them in the direction that you want them to go. In addition, you're encouraging them to speak, which makes them more likely to become engaged in the conversation. They'll probably like you more too!

6. **Listen out for 'non-sequential' information.** Always tune into this. These are snippets of information that are in the wrong order. This is when you find yourself thinking, *"I wish you'd said that earlier."* Sometimes they will reveal facts or opinions which take you off in a different direction. So, ensure you always listen attentively. You won't always accumulate all the correct information in the right order. *It reminds me of a certain Eric Morecambe quote while he is sat at the piano!*

7. **Take notes.** We have mentioned the importance of this earlier. In a confrontational situation when you aren't hearing what you want to hear, this is vital... The customer may express strong opinions. They may even come across as demanding. It is so important that everything is recorded, even in the

heat of the moment, as you may need to refer to the exact words said.

Handling objections

If you see dealing with objections as just another process, it will help you to stay in control. Sales objections, and people rejecting your ideas, are integral parts of the game. As mentioned earlier, overcoming objections, winning customers around, and turning a complaint into a resolved issue, with happy customer status restored, are some of the most fulfilling outcomes you can encounter on the phone. These, and other interactions, are some of the reasons why we choose to undertake telesales and telemarketing when many others couldn't. So, chin up and press on!

If you master this process, you will find that a customer who has a sales objection or complaint satisfactorily dealt with is likely to become a more loyal customer in the future. This may sound counterintuitive, but I've encountered many examples of this from my own experience. Plus, just think about your own attitude to a supplier in your business or domestic life who has gone out of their way to fix a problem.

If a customer likes your products or services but throws the odd objection your way, they will respond positively to your attempts to deal with these objections and help them out. Clearly, if you are flexible and can mould your solution to give the customer more of what they want, this is likely to make them happier. Equally though, they are not expecting you to give everything away. Take price matching for example. You don't necessarily have to always match your competitor's price. You simply need to explain why it's worth paying a bit extra for your product or service.

Remember, with any negative communication you get back from a customer, it's important you maintain focus on being action orientated. In other words, it's not what you *intend* to do that is important, it's the actions you carry out to resolve any issue that the customer will judge you on. Whatever else is going on, take the issue on, and aim to deal with it.

WORDS OF WISDOM

"There is no failure, except in no longer trying."
Elbert Hubbard

I offer the following mnemonic too when carrying out training. It works equally well for sales teams as it does customer service groups.

A	– Acknowledge	(let them feel listened to and understood)
C	– Clarify	(check you understand it)
C	– Consider	(think about what may work, and what you are able to do.)
E	– Explore	(discuss options, alternatives etc, find out what is important to them)
P	– Propose	(let them know what you are going to do)
T	– Timescale	(it must be done to a timescale, and both of you need to know what this is. This avoids confusion and commits both parties.)

These are important steps in dealing with negative communication from your customer or prospect. They are sequential too, sort of.

Acknowledge: This is about letting them know that you understand the point they're making. This will make them feel listened to, and that you are taking the issue seriously. *"OK, so you like our product then, but you're saying that it's a bit more expensive than what you're paying at the moment."*

Clarify: At this stage you will almost certainly be using both your questioning and listening skills. You need to make sure that you completely understand the customer's point of view. You're more likely to use closed questions at this stage to draw out a simple 'yes' or 'no.' *"OK, so what you're saying is you really like this product, but you're not sure if you'll secure the budget from your boss at the moment. Is that right?"*

Consider: You now go on to consider your options and think about where you're going to take this conversation with your customer. This is therefore essentially an internal process. This doesn't involve the customer at all, momentarily. Use some internal debate to create a couple of options for them. Then decide which one you are going to lead with. Any form of price negotiation is likely to involve this process. The customer may ask you for a discount before giving you the order. You may know what your walk-away price is, but initially you are trying to get a better price for your company.

Explore: This is where you now externalise the 'Consider' process above, placing options in front of the customer. It's all very well you considering the options, but you need to start putting them out there to the customer. Find out what may be acceptable to them. If you are in a face-to-face sale situation, you will be studying their face and observing their body language. If you're on the phone you can still listen carefully to their vocal tone, their use of language and the type of acknowledgements they give you audibly. All these things start to give you a clue as to what may be acceptable to them. Hopefully the first option that you offer will be the one they're happy with. Phew!

Propose: This is the next part of the process, where you start to put together a plan that you can agree on. Once they have agreed to an option you've put to them, you then go back over it, and summarise how it will work.

Timescale: It's important to wrap the whole thing up in an agreed timescale. Any plan needs a timeline. You are making a commitment to the process and you are turning words, thoughts and plans into action. This is important for both parties; you and the customer. It is part of the process of managing expectations too.

Talk about when you will be able to do things and when they are likely to happen. This may simply be confirmation of when you're going to call them back. It may be the part where you talk about delivery. You may start to describe the process that will happen in your company once you've loaded the order or talked to one of your work colleagues. Don't go into too much detail about the inner workings of your company. This can often end up being something that they can use to beat you with! However, what you do want to do is give them enough detail to reassure them that you know how the system works, and to help them understand why things may take a few hours, days, or weeks.

Dos and don'ts

Finally, when dealing with complaints and sales objections, there are a few principles to stick to.

1. Don't get defensive, make excuses, or ignore their point of view. Make them at least feel that their viewpoint is valid, and useful to you, if possible.

2. Don't sympathise with them: *"Oh, I know, that must be terrible"*. Instead, use empathy.

The 2 dos that you should let them know:

1. Do ensure that you fully understand their situation and point of view.

2. Do have a plan, a resolution or an idea. This must include timescales.

If you deal with customers (or in fact any of your internal colleagues too) in this way, there is no reason why every situation you deal with should not result in both parties being satisfied with a fair outcome. It may not always be a 'win-win' but we humans do at least like things to be fair. Underpinning this are feelings of respect. If we can make them feel that we're treating them respectfully and reasonably, that is often enough to build trust in the relationship.

With any form of B2B relationship, building trust is fundamental to everything that you do. I cover this topic elsewhere, but trying to go for short-term wins to the customer's detriment will usually only work once, if at all. So, if you're trying to build a long-term trading relationship with them, you need to think long-term and be guided by your moral compass. Treat them fairly, and you are much more likely to produce a steady stream of income. It feels better too.

CHAPTER 7:

BENEFIT SELLING: SELL THE SIZZLE NOT THE BACON

WORDS OF WISDOM

*"In the factory we make cosmetics,
and in the shop, we sell hope."*

Charles Revson, founder of Revlon

This is about bringing your product or service alive. Simply knowing about it and being able to communicate that clearly to your prospect or customer is only half the task.

Many of you will have had training on features and benefits. This is something talked about commonly within sales teams. And quite rightly too. It is important.

It's What's In It For Me, referring to your potential buyer, that will motivate them to buy. This is referred to as WIIFM.

If you can make them feel enthusiastic about what you are offering, it will make your selling job considerably easier. You'll start to feel positive vibes coming from them, and they will send out more buying signals as a result. In turn, this will make you more positive about what you are trying to do.

You can do this in two ways. You can grab their attention by talking about the benefits that they will get from buying your product or service. And then you can work back to talking about the features that lead to this. Alternatively, you might start talking about a feature of your latest product or service, and then go on to explain how this will give them a benefit.

In general, avoid jargon

You work in your industry or sector, and so you are likely to know a huge amount about your products and services. As a result, you are familiar with the jargon and acronyms which are commonly used. Your colleagues will be in the same position. It is therefore all too easy to assume knowledge and familiarity with terms and phrases which you commonly use. So, when talking to people outside the company, ensure you talk to them in a way that is clear and doesn't make them feel excluded.

At worst, your jargon may confuse them. Or it may belittle them and make them feel stupid. Potentially it's the 'Emperor's new clothes' syndrome. They may feel frightened to ask if they're not sure, or they may make assumptions which may not be right! This is clearly not what you want.

You may know what a 760ZXT is and does, but it is not reasonable to expect the customer to know. It is equally important not just to tell them the features of your product: *"It comes with a copper cantilever action valve"*. This is merely a description of a feature of your product. At this point, the customer may well be thinking, *"So what?"* or *"Bully for you!"*

Sometimes, jargon helps

Over the years, I have modified my view on speaking jargon. The accepted wisdom is to not get too techy with jargon and acronyms. However, I have learned that there are times when they do in fact help. This may seem counterintuitive. Just as you would use abbreviations or technical language if you're talking to a work colleague, you may well find that your customer or prospect also uses the same type of language.

If they are knowledgeable about your industry sector, then of course it makes sense to talk back to them in the same way. Sometimes, it can be a bit of a test. If they use industry terminology and you are brand new to the sector, they will soon realise this if you're not familiar with the industry sector lingo. Also, it makes perfect sense if you are talking to a customer who is knowledgeable, that you don't need to dumb down your communication to that of a beginner. Your expert customer is in danger of feeling patronised. So, while the general advice is not to baffle a customer (or particularly a new prospect) with industry language, there are times when this will be useful. The key thing is to adapt your communication style to the person that you are talking to.

FAB definitions

Feature	An aspect or technical description of part of the product or service. This is something about what it is or what it does.
Advantage	The reason the feature exists. Or how the feature works. If there was no advantage, the feature wouldn't exist.
Benefit	Why you the customer cannot do without the product or service.

Features

If you're talking about products, then features will be aspects that the manufacturer or supplier has designed in. These are intended to make the customer's life better and to help your company's products stand out from the competition. If you sell services, the same applies. It is an integral part of your service which is intended to add value.

The half-load button on a dishwasher is a feature. Heated seats in your car is a feature. Free delivery is a feature. And so is a five-year warranty. These are all examples of something about what the product or service is, or what it does. When we're selling, features are generally the things that WE get excited about.

Advantages

The next stage is to consider the advantages. These are the reasons the feature exists in the first place. If there was no advantage, then why would the manufacturer or supplier bother to include that specific feature? So, all features must have advantages. Admittedly, sometimes manufacturers seem to get carried away and include features just for the sake of it. Just because they can. It may make the product look sexier, but often we never use many of these features. One example I remember was the graphic equaliser unit on my stereo system back in the early 1990s. Initially it seemed fantastic that I could set the levels for rock, classical or easy listening. But once I'd set it all up, I never touched the levels again. I used that stereo for probably 15 years or so. And it was great! But the graphic equaliser?!

Let's return to the 'copper cantilever valve' example mentioned above as a feature. Talking about features may make your prospective customer glaze over. However, if you said to them that this feature would result in a reliable, longer lasting valve that would never need maintenance, they would more likely be interested. This statement describes advantages.

Let's consider some of the features I mentioned above.

The half-load button on the dishwasher. One advantage is that if you live on our own, you can put the dishwasher on when you are ready – to ensure you don't run out of cups or plates. *You don't have to wait until it is full.*

With the heated seats in the car, the advantage is that you can keep your bottom warm on cold mornings. These are both examples of functionality that manufacturers have put in for a reason. That reason is what we are referring to here as the advantage.

Let's consider services for a moment. A service such as Amazon Music has a feature that allows you to pay by monthly subscription. The advantage of that is that it spreads the cost for the customer.

A management consultancy may provide video tutorials as a part of the package. The advantage of this is that it allows you to access learning material at any time to suit you.

Both products and services contain features and advantages. These lead to the reasons why the customer or subscriber is prepared to pay for them: the benefit.

Benefits

The benefit is the reason why the customer can't afford to do without the product or service. This is the realisation we are trying to get them to. Let's go back to our example of the copper cantilever action valve. The benefit to the customer is that because these valves are more reliable, longer lasting and never need maintenance, they will no longer need to perform a quarterly maintenance procedure. Currently, in the customer's factory, they need to strip down the existing valves, blow them out, re-grease them and put them back together. They have 45 valves on their production line and so, because they would no longer have to perform this task, they will save a considerable amount of time.

There's only one other thing the customer wants to know – the price

The one remaining factor the customer will now want to know is the price. When your customer decides whether to buy something from you, they are consciously, or in many cases subconsciously, equating the benefit to the cost. If the customer is going to commit, the benefit must outweigh the cost. Let's go back to our copper cantilever action valve. I'll use extreme numbers to illustrate the point. If each of these valves cost one penny, providing the prospective customer believed in the claims you had made for the product, they probably wouldn't need to know much more. For just 45p they could have a complete set of these valves. They would know instinctively that this is going to save them money. Conversely, if each of these valves was £1 million, again they would be able to make an instant decision. It simply wouldn't be cost effective. They might say something to you like, *"I can see the benefit of these valves, but it wouldn't work for us. I'd be better paying Sidney our maintenance engineer to carry on performing the manual process four times a year."* They wouldn't need to reach for their calculator to work this out. Broadly speaking, if the benefit outweighs the cost, the customer will go for it. However, if the cost outweighs the benefit it will be, *"Thanks but no thanks."*

Articulating benefits

During training courses, I make the point that many products or services have benefits which are difficult to quantify. A great example is a summer holiday. We generally have one summer holiday a year, because it's a large ticket item. We don't buy a holiday simply because we don't know what else to do with our money! We know that there are other things we could spend our money on. In other words, we are *choosing* to spend our cash on the holiday rather than something else. We have decided that the benefits outweigh the costs. The benefits could include any of the following depending on who you're going with, and where you are going to.

- Chance to relax (breaking with your usual routines)

- Time with your nearest and dearest (quality time too, not compromised by daily pressures)

- Non-stop sun on your skin (if that's your thing). Beautiful weather makes you feel happier

- Exploring new places and possibly different cultures (visiting the ruins or swimming in the blue lagoon)

- Trying different food and drink. *A Greek salad with feta cheese, beef tomatoes and olives always tastes better on a summer lunchtime in Greece than it does when you try to recreate it at home, doesn't it? The same with drinking Metaxa!*

- And I could go on...

The point is that you choose to spend money on your summer holiday rather than something else. There are many benefits, and you have decided to spend the money on that rather than on something else. However, if I challenged you to work out the financial benefits of this list above, it would be difficult as there's no clear way of doing this. Plus, it would be different for different people.

WORDS OF WISDOM

"Buying shoes has become an emotional experience. Our business now is selling excitement rather than shoes."

Francis C. Rooney

I particularly like this quote of Francis Rooney's. I think there is so much more about women choosing shoes than simply buying something to walk in. Many women have a strong emotional attachment to what shoes they decide to buy, and what they wear on any specific occasion. For men, the same is often true about the car they choose to drive.

Benefits, then, are the reasons why someone will decide to part with their money. It can be difficult sometimes to distinguish between the advantage and the benefit. One way to look at it is that an advantage is the type of thing an advertiser would use in their adverts. The benefit is normally based around one of the following:

The easy to remember list of benefits
1. Saving money
2. Saving time
3. Making you look good
4. Making you feel good or giving you peace of mind

Heated seats in the car you choose is a feel-good factor. Purchasing insurance gives you peace of mind. However, that's not generally what insurance companies focus on when trying to sell you a policy. They 'suggest' the saving money element. *"Have you ever considered what you would do if your house flooded?"* They pose the question, *"How would you find the money to pay for such a one-off significant expense?"* We know that insurance companies are only in the market because they aim to make money. Which is fine of course. That's what all of us in business are there to do. If you look at a photograph of their head office, it will inevitably be a very swanky glass-sided multi-storey building. An insurance company's head office isn't a portacabin in a yard somewhere. And who's paying for this building? Yes of course it's us with our premiums. We all accept that we pay far more out in insurance than we are ever likely to claim. And perversely, we're the lucky ones! For every poor person who has their house flooded or suffers large vet bills for their poorly pooch, there are hundreds or thousands of us putting money into the kitty.

So, we are not paying insurance premiums as a financial investment. It is simply for the peace of mind that if anything goes wrong, we are covered. It's a version of feel-good – it's not about saving money.

By using Features, Advantages and Benefits (FABs) on the phone, you tell the customer not only about the product itself (which is how you see it), but also what it does for them, as well as the reason why they can't afford to do without it.

Features, Advantages & Benefits (& selling)

Using FABs is something that only happens once you are into the body of the call and are speaking to the decision-maker. Don't get involved in selling in any way to the person who answers the phone, usually the receptionist. If you are being blocked and being asked if you've spoken to your target before, you may want to refer to elements of a previous conversation. This is simply to prove to the receptionist that you are telling the truth, that you have spoken to them previously. Other than that, though, you need to keep this part of the conversation as brief as possible.

Once you are through to the decision-maker, things change. Feel free to talk to them about the new features you've added to your range of products. You do after all want to make the conversation interesting and engaging for them. Hopefully, you are enthusiastic about the range of products or services that you sell, so it makes sense to share some of this with them. But remember that, as fantastic as your features are, you must be able to turn these into benefits for the customer. While talking, be conscious of viewing this conversation from their perspective. What are they looking for? What do they want from this conversation?

And what would get them enthused? The more you can tune into this, the more successful you will be.

Landing a sale is partly about creating a situation where the next most logical thing for the customer to do is give you the order. Using FABs will help you with this. Provided you can convince the customer that the benefit outweighs the cost, you will be likely to get the order or at least a commitment. You can apply this approach to anything that costs money. Everything that you are willing to spend money on must by definition have features, advantages and benefits. If you're not sure what they are, simply ask yourself why someone would spend money on them. As soon as you start answering this question, you are starting to identify features, advantages and benefits. You can even apply this to such humble products that nature provides us with. Oranges, peas, and flowers all have features, advantages and benefits. And maybe more than most of us would initially consider.

CHAPTER 8:
STRUCTURING THE SALES CALL

Everything we have considered in the previous chapters is leading up to this: the sales call. Using the hints and tips provided, you should now have the confidence to be prepared for it.

In this chapter we consider what happens on a sales call, from the moment you get through to the decision-maker. This is the person you need to speak to. As we have mentioned, if you make a number of calls, realistically, you won't get through to the decision-maker on the majority of them. Just to help you set an expectation, I make around 20 calls per hour average. However, I average somewhere between 2 and 3 customer conversations per hour. The rest of the time the person that I want to speak to simply isn't available to take the call. On the face of it this may seem like a disappointing return on your investment. However, if your output is that you end up speaking to 10 people in a day in detail about your business and more importantly theirs, then this is still an effective way of prospecting. Especially if you're selling high ticket items. If I could find another way of managing to speak to 10 people each day who may be interested in what I want to sell, then I would consider it seriously.

Generally, you speak to a receptionist, and ask to be put through to the person that you want to speak to. In our example, Sarah Jones. The great news is, when you hear the phone answered, the voice at the other end of the phone says, *"Sarah Jones speaking."*

Let's consider how you have arrived at this point and where you go from here. I've split this chapter into 5 sections:

1. Planning
2. Opening the sales call
3. Identifying needs
4. Dealing with humans
5. Call wrap-up

Good pre-call planning creates opportunities for you. And therefore, it's an easy acronym to remember.

- **O** **Objectives.** Consider what you are trying to achieve from this call.
- **P** **Preparation.** Review the history of previous calls, what you know about this person and the organisation.

T **Timeliness.** Think about why you are calling, and where you are on the timeline.

S **Success.** How are you going to measure the success of this call?

Seeing the letters OPTS together makes me think of opportunities. So, for me, OPTS is an appropriate acronym for pre-call planning. However, often when I try this on training courses and ask the room what they think the letters OPTS make them think of, many say options. So, for the sake of this section, simply consider the opportunities you are generating. Admittedly, options probably do come into this too.

The work starts before you even pick the phone up. This doesn't mean that you need to spend ages looking up information. Certainly, if you're going to do 20 dials an hour, or even 10, it will probably mean a quick look at some history before making the call. When you get reasonably confident, you will probably be able to do this while you're dialling the number or waiting on hold. A quick flick around some of the key screens to see what the contact history is with this person and possibly what they've bought from you in the past will probably be enough.

STORIES FROM THE FRONT

Many years ago, I conducted a team audit with a prospecting team based in Warwick. This involves me sitting down with each member of the team and observing them while they make outbound calls. One of the members of their team seemed to take his pre-call planning to extreme lengths. I estimated that he was spending around 4 - 5 minutes doing some research on each company before he made the call. This would include looking at previous call notes, and at purchase history. He also had a browse around their website to learn more about them, and to get a sense of how successful they were. These weren't all cold calls. Many of these organisations he or his colleagues had spoken to before. This amount of detailed activity is largely a waste of time. As already stated, you won't get through to the person you need to speak to on most calls. Therefore, this 4 - 5 minutes is completely wasted. You will have to contact the company again at another time. Presumably, our man in Warwick would go through this whole rigmarole again. So, keep your efforts focused and relevant.

His manager, Nicola, also told me that when he had been off on holiday for a week, he spent an hour or two resetting all his call-backs for any calls with overdue dates. He set them for future dates, so that presumably he could keep his call pot tidy. Again, this activity is a complete waste of time. If you open your call pot today, having been away for a few days or even two weeks, you will inevitably have calls which are technically overdue. But it doesn't matter. You just work through them methodically to try and catch up. I'm all for having a clean and tidy database. As I've said previously, you must work hard to make sure that it contains good quality data. However, it's important to bear in mind that any CRM or database is there to support you in your phoning activity. It should never become an end in itself.

The call objective

Let's start with this. It's important to consider what you want to get out of this call. The easiest thing is to assume that your goal is always to sell, or to achieve the desired outcome. This may be to generate an appointment with a set day and date. While this may indeed be the ultimate goal of any contact with this customer, it may not be realistic on every call you make. Often, you need to settle for gaining other valuable bits of information that will advance the sales process. Learn to be happy with that. Don't get frustrated if you've not sold to somebody if that was never likely.

There are many other things that you can try to achieve. Let's consider some of them.

Your objectives may include.

1. A **sale**
2. An **appointment** for you or someone else
3. An **acceptance** of a trial
4. An agreement to a **demonstration** of the product
5. Sending **information**, either by letter or e-mail – perhaps with a link to your website.
5. **Establishing** who the **decision-maker** is that you need to talk to
6. Gathering their **e-mail address** to facilitate future contact
7. To engage in a **quality conversation** with the decision-maker which helps you learn more about them and helps them to learn about you.

I recommend that your calls should have more than one objective. You don't need to write them down or even think about them consciously. But they should be there nonetheless and be reflected in how you approach the call. Your primary objective may be to sell, to generate an appointment or to gain a booking. You should also have secondary and perhaps third-string objectives. A secondary objective may be to gather an e-mail address and obtain permission to send details through. Your third-string objective may be to find out when the budgetary process begins next, or who else is involved in the buying process, or even how much of your type of product they use per month.

Call preparation

The second element, **preparation**, is about looking up previous call notes. If these are yours, you're likely to remember them better. However, they may be somebody else's notes. Remember not to be too side-tracked by conversations that happened 3 years ago – unless they were significant. If it's a cold call, your preparation may include a quick look at their website. It may also mean reminding yourself of what was in the proposal you sent them previously, and what their buying history is.

Timeliness

Now onto part 3, **timeliness**. This is about considering where you are in the chronology of events. You might be following up a proposal. So, consider how long it is since you sent them the proposal. A week or so may be about right for something they will have to think about, and possibly discuss with others, a capital purchase for instance. However, a gap of a day may be long enough if it is a low involvement purchase. Something that they can make a quick decision on, which won't cost them much money. Remember that fortune favours the brave. Generally, you won't lose an order for following up too quickly, but you certainly can if you leave it too long! If it's a cold call you're making, then the timeline doesn't really matter too much. In fact, it's important just to get going. Start the journey with them and aim to start building the relationship. Who knows? You might just catch them at the right time.

Measuring success

The fourth and final element of pre-call planning is about **measuring success**. How will you measure it? This will be tied in with the first of our four elements - the objective. It's important to be realistic and happy with small incremental gains. For instance, if this is a cold call, you will probably need to be more modest about your expectations. Simply finding out a bit of background information and getting the name of the decision maker may be a good result. Ok, you've not sold anything to them, and maybe you never will, but you've at least started the sales journey with them. At the other end of the scale, if you are following up a proposal, then securing the order or closing the deal may be your objective. You will probably know instinctively, as you put the phone down, whether it feels like a successful call or not.

Remember that every sales call is an opportunity, even if it doesn't always look like it.

Opening the sales call

Once you have got through to the decision maker, the beginning of your sales call is critical. At this point, the person taking your call will be making a decision about whether they want to speak to you or whether they want to shut you down. Therefore, the strategy should be to try and introduce yourself quickly and succinctly.

The most professional and concise way of opening a sales call is with the three-strand intro. The opening sentence of your sales call should consist of these three things:

* Your name
* Your company or organisation's name
* What your organisation does, in one sentence

A professional telesales or telemarketing person should do this naturally. The reason it's important is that it lays your cards on the table. It indicates straightaway that you have nothing to hide, and that you're being straightforward. Additionally, it gives the call a context for your prospect or customer. They will appreciate this and be much more open with you in return. Initially, when you make a call, you know more about the call than the person you are phoning. In addition, you are more prepared than they are. So be aware that you will always get more out of them once they've caught up with you mentally.

It is certainly important that you draft your opening as a script, in your head at least. It ensures you sound confident and knowledgeable from the outset. Also, if they aren't interested in what you supply, then you want to know sooner rather than later. You can deal with this accordingly.

Back to our earlier example. Sarah Jones has just answered the phone. She is the person you want to speak to, and she has answered by saying, *"Sarah Jones speaking."* You respond by launching into your generic three-strand intro.

"Ah, good morning Sarah. It's Andrew here, calling you from ABC print and packaging. We specialise in supplying plastic packaging for the food industry." It doesn't matter whether you've never spoken to Sarah, or whether you've spoken to her many times. I think the three-strand intro is a good device to give the other person time to switch their attention to you. There may be exceptions to this. If part of your phone-based role is that of account management, and you are calling somebody on an almost daily basis, then you probably don't need to tell them what your company specialises in. Nevertheless, you should still introduce yourself and your company. It gives them the chance to disengage from whatever they were just doing mentally and focus on you and what you are saying. The good news then is that you've got Sarah's attention. Now what?

Introduce a reason statement

You now need your **reason statement**. This follows on naturally from your three-strand intro. While you're still allowing your customer to catch up with you mentally, in a few sentences explain the context for the call. This is important for the customer because it gives them an idea of what you want to talk to them about. This will help them start to decide whether they want to talk to you or not. It's equally important for you too: you should be clear about your reasons for calling as you are put through. If you struggle to give a clear reason statement, or you don't have one at all, then it probably means that you've not adequately thought about the purpose of the call, in advance. This takes us back to pre-call planning. In most cases, you'll be clear on your reason statement after looking at the company and contact name. So, it shouldn't require much thought in advance.

Some examples of good clear reason statements might be any of the following:

"The reason I'm calling you today is that ..."

"I'm calling you because it's 6 months since we last spoke, and when we spoke back in ..., you said that ..."

"I'm calling to follow up the proposal I sent you last Thursday."

"We've not spoken before, but we provide ...., and given that you are a .... type of company, I guess this is a product you use."

Reason statements are useful and powerful elements to use in the early part of your call because they indicate to the customer what your proposition is. If used correctly, your prospective customer will be happy to talk to you based on what you have said so far.

Using open questions

The third and final element of a good call opening is the use of open questions. Now you start to get into the meat of the call. You need to get the customer involved in the conversation as quickly as possible. This technique works for many reasons. The first is that we human beings like talking about ourselves. Therefore, bringing them into the conversation will start to make the process feel more engaging for them. Secondly it gives you the chance to listen and make notes about what they are saying. This will enable you to tailor whatever you say next in a relevant way. Incisive questions are a great indicator of your interest in their business, and in them personally. So, getting them talking will help you with the structure of your call and help it to flow naturally.

Ok, but what are you going to ask questions about? Most of the questions you have, fall into one of the following three categories. Most frequently they will be open questions. We considered questioning techniques in Chapter 5. The three categories of questions are:

1. **Qualifiers:** You attempt to find out quickly whether this prospect has a potential application for your products and services. And in addition, what the scale of the potential is.
2. **Research:** This is the main early part of the call. You gather relevant background information.
3. **Relationship builders:** You build rapport with the other person by talking about things which are likely to be non-work related.

There is no set order to how you should use the question categories set out above. Ideally, you merely weave these questions into the early part of your conversation.

Qualifying questions

Let's start with qualifiers. These are the questions that you want to get into as soon as possible to work out if this is a person you want to spend time talking to. That may sound blunt, even a bit brutal, but it is important to remember that you're trying to do a job, and time is of the essence. You are not trying to make friends.

If you're talking to somebody for the first time, then your qualifiers are as basic as finding out whether they use the types of products and services that your company provides. Hopefully, they do. Then you may want to find out more about the quantities or volume that they buy. For instance, if you work for a car leasing company, you may find you are talking to somebody with a fleet of 100 vehicles which are all on lease. All with varying end dates. This now presents you with a significant opportunity. In contrast, on the next call, you might end up talking to a small tradesman's business where they have two vans, both purchased. This call presents far fewer opportunities, but you are aware of this straightaway as result of asking your qualifier questions.

While I'm not suggesting these questions should be as blunt as the following examples, these are the types of things that you need to know:

"Do you buy this product or service?"

"How often do you buy?"

"What sort of quantities do you generally buy?"

"When do you think you'll next be in the market for this product or service?"

Of course, the situation is often more complex than this. For instance, if you're a tech company in an innovative part of the market, then you may have to sow some seeds first. You are looking to launch a new product or service. Therefore, by definition, there aren't many organisations using what you supply today. In this instance, your questioning will be more to do with the application that the prospective customer has. You may ask them about their industry sector or their business processes. You will seek to qualify the application. They may have a use for your product or service but right now they are unaware of its existence.

The importance of research questions

These are the most important of the three aspects of your call opening. This is because using research questions will give you a chance to advance the sales process. At this point your aim is to build up strong background knowledge about their organisation and how it operates. This is crucially important because the more you understand them, the more likely you are to spot appropriate selling opportunities. In addition, you are more likely to be able to convert these opportunities too.

Research about the company

This area of questioning further subdivides into three as well. Consider first the **company** or organisation. What does it do? What sector is it in? How big is it? And what is the company culture or ethos? Clearly, you can't ask somebody about a company's culture or ethos over the telephone. Especially on a cold call! In any case, most people you speak to would have difficulty explaining their company culture. And yet it is important. If you're in a sales role where you go to see clients at their premises, you will soak up indicators about culture and ethos just by being in the building with them. The location of their offices, the size and shape of the offices, and the number of people there, are all useful pointers. The way people are dressed, the cars in the car park, and the general state of decor are further indications of how an organisation sees itself. But it is difficult, if not impossible, to get much of a picture of this over the phone. Company culture may sound like an abstract concept but it's real, and it matters, even if it is difficult to define.

Let's consider an example. You work for a company that supplies, amongst other things, hand cleaning products. Your job is to sell your company's range of hand cleaning gels to commercial and industrial premises. You work on the phone, and so other than your general knowledge, you have little to guide you. On your next call you notice that the contact is Samantha Jones, chief buyer. The company name is Marks & Spencer, and the address is Baker Street London. Incidentally, this isn't a product that M&S would retail. Instead they would be using it at head office in the staff washrooms, and in their retail units around the country for customers.

Now, I've never sold these types of products before, and it's probable that you haven't either. But knowing something about M&S means that you will have a reasonable idea about what features of your product range you need to talk about. You might want to mention that the ingredients aren't tested on animals. You might want to talk about your sustainability policy. You might get into a good conversation about the variety of products in your range. You may well end up talking about the fact that mint and tea tree is extremely popular currently. You also supply jasmine and lemon. Not forgetting the new product - summer berries. You might want to chat about the moisturising elements of your product range. Although you can't see your customer, because you're talking to them on the phone, nevertheless you can build up a good picture of what they may be like. You may be wrong of course, but once you're into a conversation you can always fine-tune your approach.

The next company on your list is Harry Smith Motors and the address is somewhere underneath the railway arches in a big city close to you. The contact on your system is Harry Smith - proprietor. The industry type is 'car body repair shop'. And the number of employees is four. Again, you've probably built up a mental picture in your mind of what this potential prospect looks like. Here, it will be more relevant to talk about different product features. You might want to talk about the fact that you can provide your product in five-gallon drums, with an easy to peel off plastic lid. Some of the products in your range perhaps include degreasing agents and so you will want to bring this into the conversation with Harry. Equally, you will want to leave out some of the facts you focused on with Samantha at M&S. You might want to major on the fact that you provide an 'original' product which is unscented, and cheaper. And you might also want to introduce discounts for bulk buying. Harry may well want to know about the promotional offers that you have on until the end of this month.

These are extreme examples to illustrate the point. The point is that if you understand something about the company's culture, you stand more chance of making your conversation relevant to the person you are talking to. The more frequently you speak to somebody, the easier this becomes. To build up your picture about the company, you need to engage the customer in conversation. It's only by questioning them, listening, and noting key facts, that you will start to fill in the gaps, because you can't physically see them and their working environment.

Research about the person

OK, that's the company, the first category in your research questions. The second category is the **person**. Your questioning will help you build up knowledge and understanding about the person you are speaking to. It's vital to remember that although you may feel that you're trading and selling to a business, a corporate entity, it's a human being who will make the decision.

When selling on the phone you deal in one-to-one communication. Therefore, it's vital to understand something about the person who you are speaking to, and what is important to them. It's difficult at this stage to give you guidance without making some massive assumptions, but let's do it anyway. If you speak to a business owner, they may need some convincing before they will trade with you. After all, it's their personal money that they're spending. They may well want to grill you, and potentially understand all the implications of buying a product from you, especially if it's a high value item or a consultancy type service. *"What am I actually going to get from making this decision?"* they may well think.

If you're dealing with a professional buyer, you will probably find that they are not interested in the finer details of your products or services. They are not going to be using your product, and they probably won't even see it, if they work in a large company. Also, it's not their personal money, and so they may well have a highly detached attitude towards you. All they want to know is about your prices and available discounts. In many companies, buyers will be measured by the money they save their employer. In large corporate organisations, they will be dealing with many different suppliers across a diverse range of products and services. Consequently, it is easy for them to see their relationship with you and your company as merely a transaction.

If you sell to health and safety professionals, they may be interested in how your products or services help to keep them compliant. If things go wrong in their company, and there is an accident or incident on site, people will start asking some very searching questions. So, they will want to make sure that they are covered legally and have been seen to be taking all the necessary steps to protect the workforce at their company.

In my role, talking to prospective customers on the telephone about training, I deal with a diverse range of people within organisations. I frequently speak to functional heads such as customer service managers, telesales managers, or sales office managers. If it's a smaller company, I may end up talking to a director, the managing director, or the company owner. Most frequently, in medium to large companies, I will be in contact with somebody in their HR team. Or maybe learning and development if it's a larger blue-chip company. Each category of person you deal with will probably be measured and monitored on different criteria. If you are aware of what's important to them, then clearly you can make sure you steer your conversation towards the things that matter to them personally.

I don't often deal with engineers directly in my job role, but I do have a group of friends who are either engineers or come from an engineering apprenticeship background. The thing about engineers is that they always want to know *how* things work. They are less concerned about the cost of an item; it's more about the value. *"You have to pay for quality you know!"* If you sell a technical product and you're dealing with an engineer, you may be expected to know how the product works. The maintenance schedules perhaps. The carbide reinforced tip. How the product has been designed ergonomically, for ease of use by the operator.

STORIES FROM (AN IMAGINARY) FRONT

Let's imagine that you are a field-based salesperson and you sell some form of capital equipment. The type of high-ticket item which will cost thousands of pounds and will be expected to last for years. Imagine you are planning to carry out a demonstration of your product on site at a company's premises. This is a great opportunity to impress this prospective customer with what your product can do. You have two meetings lined up at the company. The first is with Steve, Kieran and Jane - the operators of the machine. So, that meeting will take place downstairs in the operational hub of the business. Then you will be going upstairs to the directors' corridor, where you have a half-hour appointment scheduled with Graham the finance director. Again, I'm inevitably drawn into making assumptions in order to make the point.

If you are demonstrating the product to the three people that will be using it on a daily basis, you need to major on the latest features. You will demonstrate how much easier this product is to use compared with the one they are currently using. It is quicker too. You may want to organise a timed demonstration of this new product compared with the current one. This is a great opportunity to impress them with how much more work they could produce in the same amount of time. If they are on some form of piece rate, where they get paid for what they turn out, pound signs may well flash in front of their eyes as they watch you do the demonstration.

If it's perhaps a product that the operator sits on or stands in such as a forklift truck, you may want to major on the latest safety innovations. The new reinforced head guard, or operator screen. The electronics have been updated as well, and so they are more reliable and now integrate with some of their other in-house systems. You have plenty you can talk about, and you are keen to show off your knowledge. This is all great. If you can orientate what you're saying to what is likely to be of interest to them, you will of course get much more buy-in. You hope that they will go back to their boss and try to persuade them that this product will improve things for their company.

You've completed your demonstration, and you're feeling good about how your new product has been received. You now make your way upstairs to have a conversation with Graham. As the Finance Director, you will almost certainly get drawn into a conversation about completely different things.

That's fine because you're well prepared. You find that you're quickly into talking about the maintenance costs of your new machine, and how they compare favourably with the existing machine. You will probably also talk about how much quicker the new machine is, so that you can reassure Graham about how much extra capacity he could gain by investing with you. He asks you questions about the finance options. What are your current lease rates on this product? And what three- and five-year long-term rental options are available? He may not want to own the product; his preference is to keep it off the balance sheet. And so, the list goes on. It's highly likely that Graham will be interested in completely different features of your product compared with the three people you have just demonstrated it to, who will be using it. So, you have focused your conversations with these two audiences on these different aspects of what you offer. You do this because you understand that they have quite different needs.

Further than this, if you try and sell the wrong features to the wrong audience, you make your selling job more difficult. For instance, if you had emphasised the lower cost lease and finance options to the three operators, they may have glazed over. It's not their money, and they may not understand what you are saying in any case. Worse than that, if you have just explained to them how much money their company will save there is a danger this could prompt the response from them, *"That's fine, but I bet we don't see any of that extra saving!"*

Equally, there is no need to go into great detail about the new more comfortable seat or controls to Graham the finance director. He's not the one using the product after all. Again, if you're unlucky and he's a hard-line boss, he may ask you what money he can save if these (presumably more expensive) comfort features were removed!

All this demonstrates that if you know something about the person you are talking to, you will naturally orientate your conversation differently. Over the phone it's much more difficult to get a clear idea about who you are dealing with, but nevertheless the more you can get them talking, the more you start to build up a picture. If you work as an office-based member of a telephone-based team, and your field-based buddy has been out to see this particular person, ensure you ask for some more details about the buyer which have been gleaned from the visit.

Build up their acquisition profile

The third and final element of our research questions is to build up an **acquisition profile**. You are interested in *how* this customer buys the type of product or service that you sell currently. If you understand their preferences, this again gives you the chance to orientate your conversation accordingly. Find out about the product or service that they already purchase, and who they buy it from. If they're a current customer of yours for some different products, this makes things considerably easier. If you understand how they operate, this gives you a good insight into their preferences. It may be that your aim is to change their way of doing things, to enable them to switch over to you. If you establish the baseline first and their reasoning, you can build the conversation from there.

If it's an item of capital equipment or a service that involves a considerable amount of investment, it is important to know how they have financed their current equipment. Do they buy the product/service outright with a one-off payment upfront? If so, they may do that to gain a good discount. Alternatively, they may be looking for finance options to pay the money off over an extended period. This may be 12 months, three years, five years or beyond. They may also not want to own the product. They may be more interested in leasing or long-term rental.

Think about your own domestic purchases and the various options which are presented to you. House insurance for instance. Do you pay for it in a one-off payment? Or do you pay it off over 12 months? If you have Amazon Prime and you also subscribe to Amazon Music, you have the option of making a one-off payment for your music which gives you 12 months for the price of 10. Alternatively, you can pay a monthly subscription. How you make these decisions personally will reflect your personality and probably your financial circumstances. It's no different dealing with corporates.

What quantities do they buy? It could be that they have a large warehouse or a considerable amount of storage space. If this is the case, they may buy larger quantities to secure higher discounts. A friend of mine who owns a couple of pet shops, frequently operates in this way. He will keep an eye on the special discounts available from his suppliers and when one particularly interesting opportunity comes up, he will dive on it and secure a large quantity of stock. He knows he can sell it at better margins over time.

Conversely, if it's a customer in a built-up urban area where space is expensive, they may be more interested in buying products on a just-in-time basis. They never want to hold much stock, and they don't want to tie up capital. They are interested though in how frequently you can deliver, because short lead times are critical to them.

Even the way people acquire things can vary from person to person. Does this customer buy online? If so, why do they do this? It's probably convenience, and it may be to do with securing good prices, but it does mean that they can't physically see the product before they purchase it. Maybe this doesn't matter to them. It also means that they need to wait for it, and with some products this may mean a wait of a few days.

In industrial markets, not everything is available next day as it is with Amazon Prime. If your business has a retail outlet, then clearly you have an advantage. Your business could be something like a local one supplying car parts. If so, you probably have a small fleet of vans who go out delivering parts on a daily basis to local garages. Again, this is a competitive advantage compared with people buying online.

Your customer may not buy online; they might choose to buy retail from a place around the corner. Or they may buy something from an industrial catalogue. In all cases, it is clearly interesting to understand how the customer behaves, and to find out a bit about why. These then, are the three areas for our research questions.

1. Company
2. Person
3. Acquisition profile

Relationship-building questions

The third and final area for our use of open questions is as **relationship builders**. These will almost entirely be non-work-related topics. This is your specific attempt to build a relationship or rapport with this other human being. Ultimately remember that

people buy from people

and so therefore you need to cultivate a relationship so that you become the *person* they want to buy from.

This is an important way of demonstrating that you are multi-dimensional, and that you have a life outside of work. This helps you to come across as more relaxed and shows that this relationship is not solely about what you are trying to sell them. You want to move your interaction away from something which is purely transactional. If you can achieve this, chances are that the customer may be prepared to pay a little more to buy from you. Conversely, if you are not able to establish a relationship with them, chances are that they will then buy from the next person who comes along. If you work exclusively on the phone from the office, your chances are more limited to develop this relationship-building early on. However, the more frequently you speak to someone, this non-work relationship will naturally build. If you've spoken to them a few times before, you may ask them a question such as, *"How was your weekend?"* You may get back an answer which tells you something about their family structure, perhaps how many children they've got, and or maybe which football team they support. If these things relate to you, then clearly you have some common ground that you can build on.

Ease into a visit

If your job role involves going to see people, then you are given more opportunities to build this part of the relationship. And you should maximise it. Typically, if you go to visit a decision-maker at their office, you will go through a set procedure. You turn up at the door and sign in at reception. Or maybe you need to press a few keys to be let into the building. Either way, you usually then wait in an area until the decision maker comes through from their office to meet you. When they do, you generally shake hands and then follow them back to their office. This is a great opportunity to talk about things which are non-work related. Don't talk about the business content of your visit until you sit down and start the meeting with them proper. So, while you're walking along the corridor, you might talk about the weather, or the road network that you've just driven along. You might comment on the building if it's very impressive, or you might start off with some general chit-chat, asking them perhaps how long they've worked at the company. Keep it light, positive, and friendly. By talking about some informal topics, you will make them feel more relaxed, and you will feel more relaxed yourself. There's plenty of time to talk about work in due course. It is likely that the meeting will start with your host offering you a drink. Perhaps they will go off to fetch this, or they may ask one of their team to do this for you. Once you've got your drink and you're both sat down in their office – you will sense that now is the time to start the business part of the meeting.

Remembering the principle that people buy from people, the more they find that you are just like them, the more likely they are to want to deal with you. Nevertheless, it's important to keep it real. Be sensitive to what vibes you're picking up from them, and don't do too much talking. Trying to ingratiate yourself excessively to a potential new customer is unlikely to help your cause. What's much more important is that you stay authentic, true to yourself. If they clearly have an interest in something which you don't, then don't try and pretend you are passionate about football, or dog breeding, or travel. Chances are you will soon get found out. Remember, people need to feel they can trust you in order to want to do business with you. If you lie about something as trivial as a hobby or interest, what else will you lie about?

In summary, your open questions are:

1. Qualifiers
2. Research
3. Relationship builders

I've outlined the structure of a good sales call. Now let's consider some practical examples.

A good sales call in practice

I often get asked, *"If you're going to keep in touch regularly, what do you talk about?"* and *"How do you open your telephone call?"*

I generally start by summarising what was said on the previous call. The first thing to be aware of is that the customer isn't ready to take your call. And so mentally they're not thinking about you and what you do. Therefore, it's a good idea to fill in the gaps and allow them to catch up with you. Also, reminding them of what was said on the last call allows you to set a context so that you can take the call where you want it to go.

> *"Hi Dave. It's Paul here from ABC Widgets. It's been a while since we last spoke – June it was. And I remember you telling me that you were looking to introduce a new line once the summer peak had gone. Tell me, how is that going?"*

Your customer Dave won't necessarily remember what was said on the last call, and he probably won't remember what their circumstances were the last time you spoke. Now that you've reminded him, it gives him a chance to catch up. In addition, by finishing your introduction with a question, you get him talking. And what's the one thing that everyone likes to talk about? Yes, it's themselves! Also, by asking Dave about the introduction of the new line, it gives him something specific to talk about. Furthermore, you're showing interest in him and his business. Which is relatively safe ground on which to start a conversation. The opening is always likely to be the most awkward. Once you've got them talking, building and developing the conversation becomes easier. The other thing that is important about getting them talking early on is that it allows you to make notes, and to think and listen to useful information. While your customer answers your question, this gives you the chance to respond accordingly.

In Dr Steven Covey's famous book, *The Seven Habits of Highly Effective People*, habit number 5 is to *"seek first to understand, and then to be understood."* This is great advice when conducting a sales call. Encouraging them to talk first will allow you to tailor what you say back in response. This makes for a much more effective and engaging conversation.

Let's consider some potential situations from that opening with Dave, set out above. One possibility is that they have postponed their plans to introduce the new line, or they've had problems with it in some way. In this instance you might want to ask how they are currently dealing with it, after you've expressed some degree of sympathy.

Sometimes, when I talk to somebody about training, the follow-up call starts with them talking to me about how business has been really tough so far this year. I have been told that they have been forced to make some redundancies. Knowing this, I now ensure that I don't go storming in and ask if they would like to spend £10,000 on a whizz-bang training solution. If I did, even if they don't say it, chances are that they would be thinking, *"Are you not listening?!"* I may still have the opportunity to ask about training, but I would tailor it to their situation. I'm certainly not saying that you should give up on looking for opportunities, but it does mean that you need to be sensitive about how you frame your questions.

The answer from Dave in our imaginary call above may well involve some sort of delay to their plans. I've started with the example of a delay as I generally find (particularly when software is involved) that this is the most common response I get. In these instances, you phone back at the agreed time only to find that they are not as far forward as they had predicted. Oh well, you simply go back to your plan.

Alternatively, things might have gone well. The new line is up and running and Dave seems positive and cheerful. After you've congratulated him, you'll probably go back to talking to him about widgets. How are things with their current supplier? What other products that you provide could they use etc?

The third possibility is that things have gone badly. They may be part-way through implementation of the new line and have experienced a series of technical issues. They've perhaps lost production, leading to some financial losses. At this point, depending on your technical knowledge, you may want to ask them about this. But keep your questioning fairly light. You don't want to come across as being judgemental. Express some degree of empathy or sympathy and, when it feels appropriate, start talking about your products again. Especially if your solution could save them money. In this instance, you are offering a benefit which relates directly to the problem that the customer has just said they are having.

In every instance, you need to relate what you say to what they've just said to you. It proves you're listening and suggests that you are on their side.

In summary then, the start of the call, once you're through to the decision-maker, should be about:

1. Giving a brief summary of what was said last time
2. Get them talking – about them and their situation

Incidentally, there are a couple of alternative openings that are frequently suggested. The first is to ask them how they are. My advice is to *avoid this* in most situations. I also suggest that this question should be directly correlated to how well you know the person. The reason that many people suggest asking your contact how they are is that this is a polite thing to do. It's human, and it's what we would start by doing when we meet somebody socially - a friend for instance.

The reason I mention the correlation is that if you ask a total stranger on a cold call how they are, they are likely to be turned off. So never ask this of a stranger. Never ever. My strong views on this are based around my own experience of how I feel when people call me in the office. I dislike it and find myself thinking, *"Just get on with it. What are you trying to sell me?"* The other reason it's a terrible question on a cold call is that they know you're not really interested in the answer. You're a total stranger and therefore how concerned can you really be? Conversely, if you talk to somebody who is a regular customer and you know them well, then yes of course this is a reasonable question at the start of the conversation. You know them as a human, and you are genuinely interested in their welfare as you would be with a friend. All of that is completely fine.

The other advice I've frequently heard is that you should ask the person if now is a convenient time to talk. From distant memory, I think that even the London-based training company who trained me and my team back in the '80s recommended it. They were excellent, and much of what they taught me I still use every day. They should also take the credit for setting me on a path that would eventually become my career. However, this is one piece of advice I dropped.

I completely understand the thinking behind this advice. It is common courtesy. By definition, if you are making outbound calls, when you get through to somebody you are interrupting them from doing something else. So theoretically it makes sense to acknowledge this by asking if they have time to talk.

Nevertheless, from a practical point of view this is a poor question. Most human beings are busy, and as we've already acknowledged, you've interrupted them. They may be irritated by this disturbance. They may be even more irritated when they realise it's you, with your sales hat on. So, instead, just get on with the call as quickly as you can, to try and change the tone of the conversation.

Another problem in asking somebody if it's a convenient time to talk is that, however you frame it, it's likely to be a closed question. One that requires a straight yes or no answer. You don't really want to give them the opportunity at the very start of the call of closing you down. Saying 'No' to you.

They are busy, and so as soon as you ask, *"Is this a convenient time to talk?"* or *"Have you got a moment to chat?"*, you are likely to get a 'No.' They weren't sitting around waiting for you to call them, so you're setting them up to just say 'No.' – You've just given them the easiest way to end the call. It means they don't have to switch off mentally from whatever they were doing when they picked the phone up to listen to you and engage in a completely new conversation.

So, you ask *"Is this a convenient time to talk?"* They respond with the polite *"Actually no, now is not good, I've got a lot on."* And that is the end of that. You don't really have anywhere to go from there. You can try to salvage the situation by asking when would be a convenient time to talk. They will answer you, but the chances are that you won't be able to get hold of them at that nominated time. In most cases they've probably given you that answer just to get you off the phone and get back to what they were doing. So, avoid this question at all costs!

Going back to what I said earlier, just start with your simple summary. This gives them the chance to mentally disengage from whatever they were doing before and start to concentrate on what you are saying. If they don't have time to talk to you, or they are really not interested in talking today, they will soon tell you! After all, they are in the position of power.

Identifying needs

Once you have engaged them in conversation, hopefully they will start to say things that you want to hear. This is the part of the call where you start to identify needs. You can only sell after you have identified and addressed the customer's needs. Ignore this principle at your peril. If you simply try to sell your product or services without properly identifying needs, you will appear pushy. It will seem that you only want to sell what you have in your kit bag, rather than what may be appropriate to them. A common complaint about salespeople is often, *"I hate pushy salespeople."* You want to come across as being professional, but not pushy. Ultimately, you're looking to build a long-term trading relationship with this other human being. Therefore, you need to play the long game.

It helps if you consider the identification of needs as having four component elements. They generally work in this order too. The four are:

1. Questioning skills (again!)
2. Matching statements
3. Benefit statements
4. Commitment

Listen!

Listening plays a key part here too. Listen carefully to the customer's language and vocal tone. When training, I generally spend around an hour talking about the impact of vocal tone, it's that important. However, this topic doesn't translate well onto the printed page. It needs to be practical and applied. Vocal tone is as important as body language is when you meet people face-to-face.

Listening to what people say and how they say it tells you a lot about what is going on in their mind. If you're lucky, they may tell you something about their needs without you having to probe too far. They may use words such as:

* Need
* Interested in
* Like
* Looking for
* Want

* We'd like

They may say something like this

> *"What <u>we're looking for</u> is a logistics partner who can ensure quicker deliveries for us."*

> *"What <u>we need</u> are four new vending machines."*

> *"What <u>we would like</u> is a new large format printer because our business is expanding."*

> *"What <u>we want</u> to be able to do is have a more agile business, and so <u>we're looking for</u> some coaching for our management team."*

As you can tell, any phrase like this will make your job considerably easier. Ideally then, you want your prospective customer to talk to you clearly about their needs. However, more usually the conversation starts with **opportunities** rather than needs. This simply means that this prospective customer may have a use for your type of product or service. However, at this stage they haven't indicated a clear desire to change from their current arrangements.

As an example, you sell a range of cleaning and hygiene products plus PPE (personal protective equipment). The person that you are speaking to works in a manufacturing environment. Clearly, at this initial stage this represents an opportunity. It's not necessarily a need, but it is an opportunity.

We are now back to questioning skills again. It's incredible isn't it, how often this comes up as being an important element of the sales process? You use your questioning skills to try to uncover needs. This is linked to the qualifying questions and research questions mentioned above. Questioning skills were covered in Chapter 5. Suffice to say, at this stage you will probably use a mix of open and closed questions. Open questions help you to identify quality background information, and closed questions help you find out whether the customer has identifiable and specific needs.

Using some good open questions will help you achieve the following:

1. You will find out more about the customer's needs.
2. You can listen out for buying signals.
3. It gives you time to prepare your response.
4. It makes the other person feel more involved.

If the customer is responsive, some good open questions should be enough to get them to open up and give you the information you need.

Using open questions should also encourage those who are unwilling to give you much detail. They are designed to open up the conversation. However, and slightly counter-intuitively, I find that if the person is proving to be particularly unresponsive, it can pay to use closed questions. Gathering some straight 'Yes' or 'No' answers may help your cause. This depends on the amount of confidence that you have. If somebody seems disengaged from the conversation, be brave to get to the bottom of it!

So you might say something like, *"We have a great range of products that are highly suitable for your application, but I get the impression that it's not necessarily something you're particularly interested in at the moment. Is that right?"*

Or you might try to be a little self-deprecating and use some humour to tease a useful response out of them. *"We have an excellent range of products that I'm sure would suit you, but I clearly haven't done a good job so far in explaining this to you, have I?!"* Sometimes this approach works, sometimes it doesn't. All you can ever do is try and do your best. And if it doesn't work, you're no worse off, are you? Provided you don't insult them by telling them that they're not being very communicative, you should be on solid ground. You may or may not feel comfortable using this approach, the choice is yours.

When I'm training telephone-based teams, I like to help them develop the habit of firing back open questions in response to almost anything that a customer says. The aim of this is to develop a mindset where you become naturally more inquisitive. Where you challenge anything that the customer says to you. The 10 statements below are examples from customers where you need to dig a bit deeper. They are of course generic, so you may need to use a little bit of imagination to fit them to your own specific application. Consider the open questions that you would ask if a customer said any of the following things to you:

1. I'm not sure we're in a position to place the order yet.
2. Delivery could be a problem.
3. I can't make up my mind which is the better product for our needs.
4. Well, if we don't get it sorted soon, we'll have problems.
5. Perhaps we could arrange for you to present your product to our head office next week.

6. Our present product is proving very unreliable.
7. But you only supply them in one colour/specification.
8. It's all got to be in place by the end of the year.
9. I'd need to check with Jack first.
10. Sorry, we're already sorted on that front. (i.e. you've missed the order)

Also consider how to frame your questions. When you're trying to narrow down the conversation to a conclusion, use closed questions. It may also help to use **positive** or **negative** questions.

"Would you like to be able to.....?" **versus** *"Does it cause you a problem to...?"*

The type of question you choose should be guided by the type of person you're speaking to. You may be dealing with somebody who is naturally positive. They're constantly thinking about growth, new ideas and developing both themselves and their business. In this situation, positive questions will probably work more effectively for you.

At the other end of the spectrum are life's pessimists. They see the glass as half empty. If anything can go wrong, it almost certainly will. This is their perception of their life's experience. If you're dealing with somebody who has this type of attitude, then probably framing your questions negatively will work better. You will get more resonance with them if you ask them something like, *"Have you considered what would happen if one of your existing machines was to go down?"* The natural pessimist will identify with this and think that this event is highly likely, if not inevitable.

Conversely this type of approach may not work with a positive person, as they may think that the likelihood is not worth considering. Of course, most people you deal with will probably be somewhere in the middle, but for the extremes the way you frame your questions can be valuable. I would imagine that if you were selling to either Richard Branson or Kim Kardashian, putting a positive spin on your questions, focusing on growth, opportunity and new ideas would probably be what they would want to hear. So, if you're ever in that situation, remember you heard it here first!

Matching statements

You've used your questioning skills to uncover needs. The next stage is to use matching statements. You use these statements to acknowledge your customer's needs, and what they've just said. This gives you the chance to reinforce in the customer's mind the ideas expressed. You then match these by introducing the appropriate features and benefits of your product or service. You are reassuring them, by telling them that your product or service will match the needs that they've just expressed.

However, there are two important things that you must do first. You need to:

- Uncover the need and
- Have a clear understanding of the need.

Otherwise, if you don't, there is a risk that you'll talk about aspects of your products or services which may be irrelevant to the customer. Your customer has just explained to you that machine reliability is particularly important to them. If one of their machines goes down, it can cost them a fortune in lost production. You may then reply with something like:

> "Yes, I understand that product reliability is important to you, and that's why we now have 500 approved service repairers around the UK."

In another instance, the customer may explain that the business is a bit fragile at the moment. As a result, they need to be careful with their budget. You consider this and respond with:

> "Yes, that's true of many companies right now, and that's why we provide a range of flexible solutions, from the 'value' range right up to the all-singing, all-dancing version. I'm sure we have a solution that would fit your current situation."

I often think that a matching statement sounds a bit like, *"We do that, we go there, I know a man who can."*

Talking benefits

You are now ready to move on to the third stage, which is to start talking benefits. These will be the phrases you use to engage the customer in conversation. If you're going to sell to them, it's important to generate some interest. You don't want them to switch off from you on the basis that they already know what you do, and what you are about to say. This can be reflected simply in some of the language that you use.

For instance, you could use any of these words when describing your products or services and their features. How about:

- New
- Exciting (only use this word if you feel comfortable with it!)
- Extended the range of ....
- Revised range of products
- An offer on until the end of ....
- Products now come with ....

On the phone, as I've already said, the other person wasn't prepared for your call and so by definition you have interrupted them from doing something else. Consequently, you only have a short while to make an impact. Remember also that the only way of getting and holding someone else's attention is by saying something interesting. Benefit statements will do this for you. The same applies if you're writing a mailshot or moving on to a different subject in a sales appointment. If you've gone through these stages of your sales call professionally and thoroughly you should now be ready for the final piece.

The commitment stage

This is often referred to as the close. This is the part which everything else in the sales process has been leading up to. The part where you ask them to buy or subscribe to your product or service. The scary bit!

However, this shouldn't be scary at all. It is a question, that is all. Don't allow it to become a big thing in your mind. I intentionally use the word commitment rather than close. This is because I think that in the sales process there are many types of commitment you can aim to get the customer to make. Persuading them to take an action that will result in them being invoiced is only one example of this. It's easy for salespeople to get fixated with the fact that on every call the aim is always to sell. In the long term, this is of course your aim. Without orders and invoiceable sales, you have no company and therefore no job. However, there are many other forms of commitment you can get from people which don't necessarily result in a direct order, but they can edge you considerably closer. Depending where you are in the sales cycle, many on this list will be more appropriate than simply trying to sell. Again, play the long game.

In fact, in many instances it won't be possible to secure an order. Nevertheless, there are things that you can do that will get you closer. Consider any of the following:

1. An invoiceable order
2. A demonstration booked
3. An appointment to visit them
4. A sample sent out
5. A trial booked on their premises
6. A short-term hire agreement
7. Sale of some consumables

As a rule of thumb, the more expensive your product or service, the lengthier the sales process is likely to be. Clearly if you're selling large turnkey projects requiring the investment of around £1,000,000, you won't sell these on the first call. Conversely, if your job is to sell paper clips, then why not just go for it?

Another reason why trying to get a commitment or trying to close somebody shouldn't be scary is that you should be expecting them to say 'yes' to your closed question. You've already identified their needs, and you've offered some relevant matching statements. So presumably you wouldn't even ask for a commitment if there were still some outstanding issues, or you felt that the customer was about to say 'no'.

By now, you should have picked up some buying signals. These are any type of statement, phrase or acknowledgement which suggests a positive response from your customer. Sometimes, they may even be aspects of body language. Admittedly, this isn't much help to you if you work exclusively on the phone. But if you're a member of the sales team who goes out to visit customers, I'm sure body language will be a key part of your sales skills. A simple smile, or somebody sitting forward at their desk when you talk about your product or services, are all positive signals.

Many questions form the basis of buying signals.

"Well, if we were to order it with you today, when would you be able to deliver it to us?" This shows that the customer is thinking about having your product. If they weren't the slightest bit interested, then what difference would delivery make?

Look out for other phrases such as *"That sounds great"* or *"What sort of credit terms would you be able to offer us for this service?"*

Buying signals may be subtle, or they may be obvious. Gestures, facial expressions, words, phrases or questions can all act as indicators. They simply show that the customer is at least thinking through the idea of purchasing your product or service. If you get these sorts of responses from your customer, then you should get ready with your commitment question. When the time is right, it's important to move ahead. If you keep trying to sell at this point, you run the risk of turning them off. And if they feel they've heard enough, they will start to disengage from the conversation. All your good work will start to unravel.

You've done the groundwork thoroughly and you now ask them the question:

"Are you happy to sign up to this then today?"

"Would you like to give me an order number?"

"Are you happy for me to put your order on the system?"

One of two things is going to happen here. They either say 'Yes', or 'No'. Let's consider how we deal with the 'No'. Hopefully, them saying 'No' will be a surprise to you. So, what do you do next? That's right – you go back to using your questioning skills again. It means that you've missed something. There is still some underlying question or concern they have which means they don't feel comfortable making that commitment.

So, although I've described this as a linear process, it can in fact be thought of as circular. Questioning, matching statements, benefit statements, then back to questioning again.

So, what's the big drama with closing? Many people shy away from trying to complete this part because they feel that they are opening themselves up to the customer being able to disagree or reject their proposition. It is the emotions of rejection that get in the way. We covered this in more detail in Chapter 6 in *Complaints, Objections and Nos*. Our natural inclination is to try and avoid such situations. But it's hardly life changing is it? Simply have a word with yourself and get over it!

Securing a commitment

A good way of giving yourself the best chance of hearing 'Yes' is to do the following two things:

- Summarise the benefits that they've accepted during the conversation
- Propose an action plan

Then request the customer's commitment to what you have suggested. The reason that you summarise the benefits first is that you are reminding them of all the reasons that they should say 'Yes' to you. You might just have had a 17-minute conversation with them on the phone and talked about all sorts of different things. You may be very aware of what the solution might look like for them, but they may not be as clear on it as you. So, it's a great idea to summarise the key parts of the call and remind them of the benefits. If you've just attended an appointment with somebody in their office, then maybe your conversation has taken an hour. You will inevitably have talked about many different things. But distil it down to the two or three key things that you believe they are interested in.

I've outlined here how to handle the 'No'. If it's a 'Yes', then you have successfully completed your job. You will be feeling happy, maybe even a little relieved. But it's important that you deal effectively with the 'Yes' as well. There is an old adage in sales which is, *"Once you've got the order you should shut up!"*

Don't take this too literally. The essence of this though is that if you've completed the selling job successfully, and the customer has just committed to you, you don't need to carry on selling at this point. The more you talk, the more you run the risk of saying something which makes the customer question the commitment that they've just given. So, be polite, bring the conversation to an end, and thank them for their time. Other than that, there should be nothing else to do.

WORDS OF WISDOM

"Show me a successful person and I will show you a salesperson. The fact is we are all selling one way or another."
Richard Denny

Handling objections

The final piece of the process to consider is dealing with objections.

Contrary to what you may believe, objections are often a good thing. They indicate that the prospective customer has at least thought about what you are offering. And, by stating a reason why they are not in a position to place an order, this gives you the opportunity to deal with it and win the business. You are at least in the game.

The best way to start dealing with the objection is to ask questions, to ensure you fully understand it. You need to listen carefully. Both these communication skills give you the opportunity to think about how you can deal with the objection that you're hearing.

If you're lucky, the objection may simply be a misunderstanding. In this case, you simply correct their misunderstanding, but without telling them that they are wrong. There are many ways you can frame this to avoid causing offence:

"Sorry, yes, I didn't explain that properly…"

"Well actually, the way it works is..."

"Okay well the good news is that..."

"Well actually, it's better than that because..."

You may well go back to setting out some benefit statements to reassure them.

More commonly of course, their objection is specific. They may tell you that your price is too high. Or more expensive than what they're paying currently. They may tell you that they are happy with their current supplier. They may tell you that something about your offering doesn't quite fit their needs. Maybe your lead times are too long. Maybe you don't provide a product or service that quite meets their specification. If you perform any form of sales role, you will have heard all of these (and more) many times before.

Let's consider the old classic, the price objection. Let's assume that the price you are offering is more expensive than one of your competitors. Your product sells at £449; their product is £399. Which product is the customer going to choose? The simple answer is that if both products (or services) look the same to them, they will of course opt for the cheapest. Why would anyone pay more for something when the two products look the same? Clearly then, you need to differentiate your product from your competitors. You need to point out to the customer that these two offerings are not the same.

A useful tactic here is to sell the price difference, not the whole price. They have almost certainly committed to spending the £399 – mentally at least. All you need to do is explain what they will be getting for the extra £50. It's considerably easier to sell the £50 difference than it is to sell the whole price. From this point on, do not even mention the full price. Just keep talking about the £50. By doing this, you lessen the impact of the difference between your competitor's price and yours. You explain all the benefits the customer gets by coming to you. This could be features and benefits of the product or service, and/or it could be things relating to what you provide as a company in the way of support. You will find that it's easier to overcome this objection in this way. On the face of it what looks like a fairly significant difference actually comes down to just a few pounds. Ultimately, most customers want a reliable product or service. Some will always buy on the lowest price of course. But the majority are generally looking for value. What do I get, and what will it cost to me?

STORIES FROM THE FRONT

Many years ago, our daughter was about to celebrate her 21st birthday. She was studying at Sheffield, and therefore we were going to have a night out in the city. The idea was that my wife, our youngest daughter (aged 10) and I were going to make the 90-minute journey to Sheffield on the Saturday. The plan was to take our 21-year-old daughter and her boyfriend out for a meal in Sheffield. We decided that we would look for a hotel for the night. We wanted a family room that would accommodate the three of us. We didn't know Sheffield particularly well, but we knew of a few hotels around where our daughter lived in Broomhill. We remembered one specific place which looked like a medium-sized but independent hotel, and we agreed that this would be suitable accommodation.

My wife made the call and found that they had available family rooms for this Saturday night in February. She came back and told me the price, £120, and we agreed that it would fit the bill. Nevertheless, I wondered whether we could get something else similar at a lower cost. My reasoning was that we wouldn't really be using the facilities of the hotel. We would simply travel up on the Saturday afternoon, dump our bags, have a wash, and prepare to go out for the evening. So, we needed something comfortable and clean, and somewhere that would do us a good breakfast the following morning. We would then pack the car and head back south. With that thought in mind, I asked my wife if she could perhaps find something for let's say £100.

She did a bit more research and found us a place with an available family room that would accommodate the three of us for £100. Job done. We booked and looked forward to the Saturday night out with our daughter and her boyfriend.

We made the journey up on this February Saturday and checked into the hotel mid-afternoon. The people who ran the place seemed very friendly, and we looked forward to our evening ahead. However, we weren't blown away by the place. The building was an old Edwardian or Georgian building and clearly needed a bit of investment. It looked a bit tired. Our room was much the same. Being an old building, it had a high ceiling. The small and old-fashioned radiator was never going to be adequate to heat this large space. And remember this was February. Furthermore, some of the wallpaper was peeling off the walls slightly, and I noticed that the mirror above the wash basin had gone brown in places.

We set out to walk to the restaurant in the early evening. We had always planned to walk because we were going to drink. We'd been walking for around ¼ hour when we happened to walk past the other hotel I'd rejected for £120. Bearing in mind this extra 15-minute walk, which we would have again on the way back of course, meant that we had an extra half an hour of walking in total. My wife wasn't making any particular issue of it, but she did casually turn to me and say, *"You do realise don't you that for an extra £20 we could have been staying in there tonight?"* And that for me was one of those 'Doh' moments. That really was the nub of it. I'd simply made the decision to save £20. And in the great scheme of things how significant was that £20? We could have stayed somewhere that saved us half an hour walking and was possibly a bit more modern inside. When I looked back at the decision afterwards, I learned an important lesson. It's all about the difference, not the full price. Use it to your advantage.

OK, back to dealing with an objection. It will go one of two ways. If you're able to do something directly about the objection you are facing, then that is probably the most effective way of combating it. In the example of your price being too high, you will explain what they get for the extra money. You will aim to justify this price increment. If you sell some form of commodity, and it's difficult to do this, then you may need to look for some form of creative pricing. However, you want to avoid simply trying to price match at the first opportunity. This generally results in a race to the bottom, where you may win the account in the short term, but you will lose it again when somebody else comes along offering a lower price than you.

In the example I gave of your lead times being too long, maybe you should check how many they need right now. You might not have enough in stock to fill the whole order, but maybe you could supply some of them now quickly, with the rest to follow. Would this work for your customer? There are many creative solutions you can come up with depending on the set of circumstances you're dealing with.

Finally, if you can't directly address the objection they have, you need to try a different approach. You remind them of the benefits of buying your product or service. You do this to put forward benefits which outweigh their objection and preferably relate these benefits directly to their objection.

For example, if the objection you face is around price, then reminding them of lifetime operating costs, or reduced maintenance costs, may help your cause. The case you present may revolve around the fact that they are spending £2,000 more now, but that they will save £6,000 to £7,000 over the next three years, due to these lower operating costs. You relate the benefits you talk about to what they say is the reason they don't want to buy from you currently. And if you are not able to do that, you just need to throw some of the other key benefits at them in the hope that these will outweigh the price objection in their mind. Some you will win; some you will lose. But at least you've had a good go at the order. If you don't win at this point, there is probably little else you could have done. And if you don't win this order, immediately start talking to them about other future opportunities. If there aren't any, at the very least, agree to keep in contact with them so that you can keep the dialogue going. This is positive action, which will help you position yourself to win orders in the future. And remember

"If you can't be number 1, aim to be number 2."

The final piece of advice is around ring-fencing objections. This is something that I've experienced being used on me. I've also read about it in a sales article.

Let's assume you feel confident, and believe you are about to receive an order from your customer. However, they come up with an objection which on the face of it they think you cannot directly do anything about. If you are confident that you possess the ability to combat it, it's important to find out if this is the only thing stopping the deal going ahead. You want to call their bluff, and check that this isn't simply an excuse. So, in this instance, you try to ring-fence the objection with a question like this.

> *"OK, I understand. And is that the <u>only</u> thing that's stopping you going ahead with us at the moment?"*

If you are confident that you can address this, you are in a strong position. As soon as they say 'Yes' you can respond by saying that you will work on addressing that *one point*. This will clear the way for you to secure the order. If you don't ring-fence the objection, you run the risk of simply running into a barrage of excuses. So, for instance, you offer to reduce the price, and they still don't commit to you. They come up with some other reason why they won't move forward. In addition, if you put considerable time and effort into overcoming this objection, such as going back to your company and talking to work colleagues in stock control or pricing, you don't want to find that this work has been in vain. Ring-fencing will hopefully help you identify whether this is a genuine objection or merely a smokescreen.

STORIES FROM THE FRONT

I do a bit of cycling over the summer months. I do admit at this point that I'm a fair-weather cyclist. I generally start getting interested around Easter time, and put the bike away in mid-September after a big weekend away. I enjoy the exercise and I like breathing in the English countryside air. But I'm not a diehard cyclist and see no attraction in being out in the cold or rain. Just saying.

Many years ago, two old school friends of mine from London, Mike and Steve, put forward the idea of having a boys' weekend away cycling. This was intended to be a proper adventure over a couple of days in a different part of the UK, which involved camping. I can't remember the precise details now, but the idea was that we would travel 100 miles or so and much of this would be on tracks, along lanes or off-road.

I said to Mike that I thought it was a great idea, and sure - I'd like to come along. However, as Mike knew, I didn't have a bike. This was my reason I wouldn't be able to join in. You would have to agree that that is a fundamental objection isn't it? He asked me if I knew anyone who I could borrow one from, but I didn't feel comfortable with this. Even if I could find somebody, I wasn't sure that riding it for 100 miles or so over hills and dales would necessarily be very fair. So, the conversation ended there and nothing much happened until the following year.

This time it was Steve who made the call to me. He said, *"Look Andy, we had this idea last year, but we never went ahead with it. Wouldn't it be a great idea to get a group of us lads together for that cycling weekend away?"* I came out with the same objection I had offered the previous year to Mike. I said, *"Yes it sounds like a lovely idea, but I won't be able to do it because I still don't have a bike."*

He then asked me, *"Is that the **only** reason you can't make it?"* And I said *"Yes, it sounds like a great idea."* He replied quickly with, *"OK great, I've had a word with my brother Stuart and he's happy to lend you his bike."* And so, it happened. I used Stewart's bike and had a great weekend away with the boys, and a couple of girls as well. It was the South Downs Way, and boy was it tough?!

The same happened the following year. We cycled somewhere else. After that I thought it was a bit unreasonable to keep borrowing a bike and so I bought my own. The annual bike ride has been a longstanding tradition in my life ever since. The original group evolved into the same six guys cycling around some fantastic parts of Britain at the beginning of September every year for six years. That group split, and so I formed my own group of local friends. And we've now been cycling, with the same group of us, for 12 years. Incidentally, I still use the same bike, so it's been remarkably good value - my trusty Giant hybrid.

There are two things we can learn from this story. The first thing that Steve did was to ring-fence my objection. As soon as I trotted out my reason for not being able to come along, he checked to find out if that was the only thing stopping me from going. Furthermore, he already knew in advance what I was going to say. So, he was ready for the objection. The second thing that he did was pre-handle it. Because he knew what I was about to say, he had done some preparation to make sure that he could overcome it. He had had the conversation with his brother and obviously asked if his mate Andy could borrow his bike for the weekend. Once his brother Stuart said yes, he knew he had a good chance of getting me to commit.

Pre-handle objections

This is a non-work example, but I believe that you can pre-handle nearly all the objections you will ever face. My belief is that once you've worked in a sales job within an organisation for, let's say, 12 or 13 weeks, even by then you will probably have heard 95% of all the objections you will ever hear. Consequently, just put in the spade work to make sure that you're ready for them.

As soon as somebody trots out a particular reason why they can't trade with you at this time, in your head you should be thinking something like, *"Oh, OK, here we go – this is reason number 9. And when I hear reason number 9, I then respond with this."* And have whatever statement or phrase you use ready. There isn't much that should catch you out, and so therefore you can always be prepared. On this basis, I believe that sales objections shouldn't really cause you too much hassle. Very, very occasionally, you may get somebody who throws something at you that you've never come across before. In this case it will probably unnerve you, and you may not deal with it as well as you could. But that's fine, simply go away and find out. Perhaps from your manager or a work colleague, how you should deal with this new objection. That way, you simply add it to your internal mental knowledge base, and next time it comes up, you're ready for it!

Call wrap-up

Once the call feels like it's coming to a natural end, you now conclude with the highly important call wrap-up. You will learn to know instinctively when you're at this point. The conversation dries up, and you feel that you've stated all the key things that you need to cover. It's equally important to pick up cues from your customer as well. If you're sat with them in their office, then be aware of their body language. If they start to go quiet, and stop asking questions, that may be an indication that they feel the meeting is over. Another classic sign of their attention being elsewhere is if they look at their watch or the office clock. If either of these things happen, you need to bring the meeting to a swift conclusion.

Over the telephone of course, it's much more difficult to pick up these vibes, but they will be there anyway. Again, if the customer seems less engaged in the conversation, and all the major aspects have been covered, this indicates that they are ready to move on to something else. Don't irritate them by wittering on too long. And certainly, don't go into full-on sales mode either!

It's important that you keep as much energy, concentration and focus at the end of the call as you did during the earlier parts. In process terms, the call wrap-up should consist of three things:

1. Summarise – the key point or points
2. Agree the next action – and when with a reason
3. Thank them for their time

Summarising the call

This is a great way of setting some context around what the next action will probably be. It is your chance to remind them of the highlights of the call, and what you have talked about. It also demonstrates that you are professional, and that you have taken the conversation with them seriously. You may read back from notes, and this shows that you understand what the conversation has been about. Certainly, if they need to perform some sort of next action such as sending you a specification or giving you a purchase order, then your summary helps to remind them why they need to do this.

Agreeing the next action

Always put forward a clear next action for yourself too. This is you subtly asking for permission to keep in touch with them. For any account, whether they are buying from you or not, you should aim to have some future contact. Your next action shows your commitment to keeping in touch with them, regardless of what has happened on this call. The conclusion of the call may have varying degrees of positivity. For example, you may put forward one of the following next actions

"OK, well I'll give you a call back in September then, after the summer shutdown and we can chat about your plans for the last quarter."

"OK, so you've got no budget at the moment, but I'll catch up with you again in January then, when your new budget comes through."

"Great, well I'll check availability with our suppliers, and I should be able to come back to you in an hour or so, and let you know when we could get some of those over to you."

Thank them

Finally, it's important to thank them for their time. This is a respectful act and will leave a positive impression with them as the concluding thing you say. It's important to recognise that we're all busy, and this other person has been prepared to give you some of their time. It might have been a meeting in their office, or perhaps an 8- or 10-minute conversation on the phone. Either way you simply acknowledge this and thank them.

After the meeting/call

This is where your direct one-to-one communication with the customer or prospect ends. Your job still isn't quite done yet. There is one final thing to do. It's important that you now update your system. This becomes a crucial piece of information which will help you in all aspects of managing this relationship with the customer in future. So, it's important to do it while it's all still fresh in your mind. If you're working on a screen, fill in all the key details, including your call notes. Then press save. The main reason why the quality of call notes is so important is that this will be the raw material you will use when making your next contact. The better-quality notes you have, the more confident you will feel going into the next call. Good quality, detailed notes prevent your subsequent contact feeling like a cold call. So, input them, and then reread them for accuracy. Once you've done this, and you're happy with it, you're now ready to move on to whatever you're doing next. This could be the next call, or it could be to take a break or make the coffee.

You've successfully completed all the action points of a professional salesperson, so now you can move on to your next action with a clear conscience and no need to rely on your memory - everything is safely documented.

WORDS OF WISDOM

"Nothing happens anywhere in the world until a sale takes place. And salespeople bring in the money that everyone else can live off."

Richard Denny

CHAPTER 9:
GETTING PAST THE GATEKEEPER

As anyone making outbound prospecting calls knows, gatekeepers stand between you and glory! Telemarketing and telesales jobs would be so much easier if only the receptionists, PAs etc would put us through to the decision-maker. However, you simply need to see this as an occupational hazard. So, you need to develop ways of dealing with it. And probably even more importantly - not let it get to you.

Respect the imbalance of power

Most of the time it is easy to consider the receptionist who asks you loads of questions as someone who is there simply to make your life difficult. They stop you getting the sales process going. You're not even out of the blocks.

I've worked with many telemarketers over the years who consider this first point of contact as the devil incarnate. They disrupt your flow by asking you questions such as:

- What's the call about?
- Are they expecting your call today?
- Has he/she spoken to you before?
- Is this a sales call?
- Who is calling?

These are all objections of a type, and you're not even through to the person you want to speak to yet. So, it is easy to think of these gatekeepers as your adversary: someone you need to beat to get to where you want to go. Maybe even someone you need to find a way to trick to get past. Avoid this thinking.

The reason for this is that in this relationship, they hold the balance of power. It may be tough to admit this to yourself, but they do! You must respect the fact that they are in the position of power. Therefore, they can decide whether they will put you through – or not. Let's consider the situation from a different perspective.

The gatekeeper as your friend

Your first aim should be to create a positive relationship with them. Or perhaps more realistically a neutral relationship. In other words, one that isn't negative. You are likely to get far more from them if they feel well-disposed towards you. It's important to remember that they are just doing their job. They are specifically asked and expected to field out unsolicited phone calls. So, you need to respect this. In the same way that your manager doesn't want to receive too many calls, it is the same with the person you are trying to get through to. If you accept this fact, you will be more likely to treat them respectfully.

So, contrary to them being an obstacle, see them as someone who can help. You will often be surprised. If the person you are trying to reach is notoriously unobtainable, you can always ask the receptionist or PA when the best time is to get hold of them. Remember to use words like advise, help, suggest. People naturally like helping, and so you can ask them when they *suggest* you should call next. Of course, even if you think that the decision maker is avoiding taking the call, you can always give them the benefit of the doubt by saying that you appreciate they're busy.

> *"Yes, I understand that Geoff is busy, but when would you suggest is the best time to get hold of him?"*

It won't work all the time of course, but it may work some of the time. And often this is all we need in selling – small incremental gains.

WORDS OF WISDOM

"You may be disappointed if you fail, but you are doomed if you don't try."
Beverley Sills

Maximising call value

It is also important to gain some value from as many calls as you can. In other words, try to add to your own knowledge, by making sure that you know more by the end of the call than you did at the beginning. So, ask the receptionist for other people who are also involved in purchasing or specifying the products or services you supply.

Even if these people are not the main decision maker, often another contact will give you good background information. Or at least they can give you an idea about how good a prospect this organisation really is. How many times does it happen that you pursue somebody for days, weeks, months, or years only to find that they're not the real decision maker? Alternatively, you may find that, once you've spoken to them, that they seldom buy the types of products and services you sell. This is immensely frustrating, and I need to hold my hands up, and say I've done this many times! You have now wasted a large amount of time and mental energy. Simply put it down to experience and view it as just another part of the job.

So, build up information from as many people as you possibly can within the organisation. Also, remember to support this effort by making a note of every decision maker that you speak to. You will often need to speak to them again in the future, for example, if your main contact leaves, and so making a note can be invaluable.

If you phone up one day to speak to Sarah Jordan and you are told that she has left the organisation, you now have some other options. You have previously spoken to her PA,

Jane Summers, and so you ask to speak to her instead. This allows you to glide into this new conversation with ease.

> *"I know we've spoken a few times before, Jane, when I've been trying to get hold of Sarah. Obviously, I've just been told that she's now moved on, and so I'm interested to know if someone else has taken on her role yet."*

You have at the very least made this sound like a warm call. As I've said elsewhere in this book, using knowledge and information limits the amount of truly cold calls you have to make. Always be prepared to ask people what they know. Another benefit of gathering information from various people is that it helps you build up a more accurate picture. Much of what anyone ever tells you will be just their opinion of course. That's entirely natural. Consequently, if all your knowledge about a particular prospective account is based on conversations with just one person, some of it may be misleading. If, however, you have spoken to two or three people, you may have built up a more accurate overall picture.

Make it a warm call

Outbound cold calls are often more difficult than warm ones because you have no track record with the company or person you are calling. So, it is important to make sure that repeat calls don't sound like cold calls. This means noting as much relevant information as you can from previous calls, so that you can 'prove' to the receptionist that you have called before. If you have spoken to the decision maker before, and the receptionist is giving you a hard time, you can always feed them a little piece of information that your target contact told you previously. Generally, if you have spoken to someone before, the receptionist will at least go off and ask them if they want to take your call.

> *"Yes, when I spoke to Miranda six months ago, she said that she wasn't looking at it at that time. But she did say that once her new boss started, she'd be interested in talking to them about it."*

Or perhaps:

> *"Kieran said that things were a bit tough back in May, and I know you made some redundancies in the factory. But he did say he'd be interested in talking to me again once the new budget came through in October."*

As you can see, in both these examples, the receptionist is now clear that you have spoken to your contact before. So, they are likely to at least go away and talk to the decision-maker for you. Chances are that if the contact remembers you, they will probably take your call as well.

Even if you haven't spoken to them before, you may have found out about the products they use, or the hours they work. Again, you can use this information to make it sound like there has been previous contact.

> *"Ok, I understand that she's in a meeting at present. I believe she finishes at 2:30 each day, doesn't she? So, in that case I'll try again tomorrow."*

Be human

The most important thing that will decide if a receptionist or PA wants to help you is whether they like you. So, it's important that you aim to come across as a warm, friendly human being. A bit of idle chatter on occasions will help too. I also find that you will normally get away with gently mocking them when they say, *"Good afternoon"* when they meant to say, *"Good morning"*, with a phrase like, *"Now that's somebody wishing their day away!"* After all, they like to feel that you're human like them.

You also need to come across as relaxed and friendly. You absolutely mustn't come across as being desperate to speak to your contact. After all, you're successful and have many active accounts on the go right now, don't you?! So, if they won't put you through, you accept it with good grace. The alternative really won't help you. Also, be aware of your vocal tone. This is really important, but not a factor I've attempted to address in this book. Principally because it is highly nuanced. Although I cover this as one of the cornerstones of my classroom-based training, it is difficult to convey when using only the printed word. Aim to come across as being bright and breezy, and make sure that you have energy in your voice. You don't want to sound like yesterday's leftovers.

When I'm carrying out the advanced training course, we normally include a lively interactive session where we consider ideas to get past the gatekeeper. Because my audience is a group of people who deal with this daily, they always have plenty of ideas. Here are ten of the best ideas which these sessions have generated:

Getting past the gatekeeper

1. Try calling your contact at one end of the day or the other, when the receptionist is unlikely to be there.
2. Always store direct dial numbers when they are given to you, or you hear them on voice mails. *So, always be ready with pen and paper.*
3. Go via another department, accounts for example.
4. If you don't have the name, try the two-call approach.
5. Name-drop other people.
6. Default to other methods of contact. *E-mail for instance.*
7. Use some technobabble, or legalese; technical information that the receptionist doesn't feel confident answering for them.
8. Refer to previous history such as orders, contact, conversations (especially if the decision-maker you previously dealt with has left.)
9. Use related reference sites. This is useful where there is a degree of industry specialisation.
10. Ask for them by name: directly, assertively, and confidently. You could also simply ask for them by their first name if appropriate.

Most of these are self-explanatory, but here are a few additional comments, using the numbered points above.

Point 1: The receptionist doesn't work all the time

They take holidays and will inevitably have breaks during the working day. Therefore, it's a good idea to try them at a time when they may not be there. So why not try them at either end of the working day? If you get lucky you can sometimes get through to a company even before the switchboard is open. Somebody else just might pick up the phone.

Point 2: Storing contact numbers

Often, you will hear other phone numbers mentioned, such as their direct dial number. It's always a good idea to keep a note of these. You may be given their mobile number, especially if they are somebody who has a national role and is seldom in the office.

I must admit that I'm not keen on using mobile numbers. I always prefer to contact someone at the office if I can. I don't like the idea that you could phone somebody in the middle of doing something else completely non-work related. They could be sat in the dentist waiting room; they could be in the queue at Tesco; they could be sat at home taking a 5-minute break with a mug of coffee in their hand. I really don't want to disturb any of these situations with my call.

However, I acknowledge that in the modern business world many people are glued to their mobile phone. And certainly, if somebody has a national role, then they almost certainly receive all their work communication via their mobile. I do understand all of that, but I'm still not comfortable with it. However, don't let my prejudices affect you.

Point 3: Going via another department

This can often be an effective way of bypassing the gatekeeper. So, for instance, you phone a company, and commonly you will hear a series of push button options. Commonly, option 0 is to speak to the receptionist. But you've spoken to them a few times, and you're getting nowhere. Why not consider choosing one of the other options next time? It depends what your product or service is of course, but for instance you could try option 3 for accounts. Once you're through to the accounts team, you simply ask for Jenny Harper as you would do in the normal way.

> *"I was looking for Jenny Harper. Do you know if she's about?"*

Now, at this point Jane in accounts doesn't know how you've ended up with her. And in most instances, she probably isn't going to be bothered trying to work it out. The call clearly isn't for her, and frankly she doesn't want to get involved in a detailed conversation with you. So, frequently she will just say, *"OK, I'll check"*, and she will attempt to put you through to Jenny Harper's extension. Another department that may be equally helpful might be HR. But as I say, this does largely depend on what product or service you sell. Try operations or the warehouse, but not if you're trying to get hold of the M.D.

Point 4: The two-call approach

I have found that this is the most effective way of trying to contact someone when you don't have the name. In the early days of telemarketing back in the 1980s, we were all trained to ask for, *"the person who deals with buying all your stationery,"* or *"the person who specifies all your PPE."* However, this makes it obvious that this is a completely cold call. You may well be lucky and get through. But if there is one type of call that is likely to be blocked, this is probably it. Therefore, if you don't have the name of the person you want to speak to, and you've exhausted all avenues such as LinkedIn, you could try the two-call approach. You make the first call and say who you are, and the name of your company. You explain that you're going to send some information through. You don't even have to specify whether this is by email or post. So, you might say, *"Good morning, my name's Phil, and I'm calling from ABC Print and Packaging. I'm about to send some information through but could you tell me who's in charge of your print and packaging please?"* In this example I've kept the wording brief and pretty vague. In my experience, they are likely to give you the name of the person that you need. You simply thank them for their time and end the call. If the receptionist seems chatty, friendly and open, you might want to push your luck and ask for their email address. It's your judgement call. But at the very least if you can finish this brief call by gathering the name you need you are considerably further forward. And remember what I've said elsewhere, this is all about incremental steps.

You then leave it a few days, or even a few weeks, and you phone back. At this point you now simply ask for the person by name. *"Good morning, can I speak to Jordan Vince please?"* You may or may not have sent information through in the meantime. But for the sake of this call, it doesn't matter either way.

Point 5: Name-drop other people

Clearly, if you have had a conversation with somebody else previously and you've got a name, then your job is considerably easier. The most powerful one is if you've been given the name of the decision maker by a more senior person. You might have met the sales director George Harris at a networking event or a trade exhibition. If he told you that it's Billy Parsons the production manager that you need to speak to, then you seek to use this information on your call. You phone the company and ask for Billy Parsons. The receptionist asks you what the call is about, or who you are. *"OK, my name is Paul Thompson, phoning from KLM workwear. I had a conversation recently with George Harris and he suggested that it's Billy Parsons I'd need to speak to. Could you put me through please?"* At the very least, she is likely to go off and ask Billy if he will take your call. And the chances are that if you've been speaking to George Harris, one of the directors, he probably will.

Whilst that is ideal, you may only rarely be in this situation. At the other end of the spectrum you might have been scouring LinkedIn for some contact names. You might not be able to find the name of the person you need. You've managed to get some other names, but they're not in the department that you want. Let's consider that you want to get hold of somebody in Learning and Development. You can't find any details, but you do perhaps have the name of somebody in HR, Kelly Rothery. The LinkedIn profile suggests that they may be somebody junior. Their job title is HR Assistant, and their thumbnail picture looks like they're fairly young. But if this is all you have to go on, you could at least try it. You have nothing to lose. So, you get through to the receptionist and you ask to speak to somebody in Learning and Development. You get blocked with the question, *"What's the call about?"* So, at this point you simply say, *"Well, I've got the name of Kelly Rothery here, but I'm not sure. Is she the person I'd need to speak to about learning and development?"* Now, you know that she is almost certainly not the person. But at this point, it sounds to the receptionist as if you've had conversations with somebody before. In this instance, she is more likely to correct you, and say, *"Oh no, it wouldn't be Kelly, it would be Sarah Jarvis."* You still don't know Sarah's role in the company, but at least you now have a contact to aim at. You ask to be put through.

Point 6: Alternative methods of contact

If the receptionist blocks you by saying that Jackie Smith doesn't take sales calls, you then simply ask if you could send her an email instead. You will often find that this works. At this point, I strongly recommend that you do send Jackie an email. You are at least introducing you and your company to her, and on the very slight chance that she might be in the market at the moment for your products or services, at least it puts you in the frame.

The other thing that might happen is that the receptionist won't give you Jackie's email address, but she will give you hers, with the promise that she will forward your email. You then need to thank her and come across as being warm and genuine. You promise that you will, and you *do* send the receptionist your introductory details for her to pass on. The same day. It will be a template after all. She may well pass it on, but of course you don't absolutely know. But it almost doesn't matter. You have just made considerable strides forward. You've managed to send some introductory information which may end up with person who you want to read it. Of course, the real gold nugget is that you probably now have the decision maker's email address by default. If you know the receptionist's email address, you now know the format of the company's emails. So next time around, you can always try emailing Jackie directly. Admittedly, there are many ways of spelling Jackie, Jacky, Jacqui, and so you may have to try the same email a few times. But it doesn't matter, because the ones that are wrong will bounce and so nobody at the company will ever know that you are fishing for the right spelling. It's your little secret.

Point 7: Using technobabble or legalese

This will entirely depend on which industry sector you are in of course. For many of you this won't be an option. But if you sell products or services that are based around health and safety, financial services, or anything to do with compliance, then you have some added opportunities.

You don't need to enter into a detailed conversation with the person answering the phone, but you do want to make them hesitate before blocking your call.

> *"In the light of the new legislation around blah-blah, I just wanted to chat to him about how your company is going to work with these new rules."*

Or you could possibly use:

> *"There are some hefty fines now for companies that break this new rule. I just wanted to update her on this and see if I could help."*

In these types of situation, you may be saying enough to make the receptionist think that they shouldn't take the risk of not putting you through. Again, at the very least, they are more likely to go away and ask the person if they want to take your call.

Point 8: Refer to previous history

Doing this can give your call more credibility. This is perfect to use if the decision maker that you used to deal with has now left the business. In this instance, try something like this:

> "Yes, I used to deal with Valerie. And I know that she was keen on our products and wanted to look at them in a little bit more detail after the summer."

Or when pursuing your usual contact, you could say:

> "You've bought lots of our XYZ product over the years. Is Steve available please?"

Point 9: Use related reference sites

If you work in a niche industry sector, you can use this to your advantage. You can mention that you deal with company X, and then insert the name of the large company on the edge of town that the people in this company will almost certainly have heard of. It could be a large employer in the same sector, or it could be a likely customer or supplier to this business that you're talking to. The aim here is that if you can promote the idea that you have some degree of specialist knowledge in their industry sector, they are more likely to want to engage with you.

For instance, if you provide engineered components to the automotive industry, then being able to say, "Yes, some of our products are already used by Mercedes-Benz and Jaguar" may well help your cause.

Point 10: Simply ask for the person

Avoid any hesitancy, and just be direct and assertive in asking for the person you want to speak to. Make sure that your vocal tone sounds confident. Depending on the type and size of company you're talking to, you can sometimes just ask for the contact by their first name. Clearly, you need to exercise some common sense. If you're phoning a company with over 500 employees and you ask for John, you won't get very far. If the person has an unusual name though, it is easier to try this. There is a ceramics company I contact from time to time. The director that I generally speak to is Geoffrey. The company isn't massive, and therefore when I phone them, I always simply ask for Geoffrey. Never Geoff, but Geoffrey.

WORDS OF WISDOM

"Deep down, we believe that the problem put simply is THEM. They, of course, believe WE are the problem."

Unknown

Don't be phased by dealing with gatekeepers. See it as part of the game. Remember, they are simply doing their job, just as you are trying to do yours. Adopt a relaxed attitude and use your natural powers of charm and persuasion to engage with them. If that doesn't work, use some of these top tips here to get around them.

CHAPTER 10:
CLIMBING THE SUMMIT

Although I've written this book and have pursued a career in telesales and telemarketing, I would be the first to acknowledge that making outbound prospecting telephone calls isn't easy. In their attitude to the prospect of this task, most businesspeople divide into two camps. Those who have never done it but reckon that it looks easy. And those, probably the majority, who look upon it as either too difficult, or something that they would do their best to avoid.

The mechanics of making prospect phone calls are in fact easy. You simply make some telephone calls and try to speak to people about your products or services. You probably know a great deal about your products and services, and so therefore in theory this should be quite straightforward. And if you don't have success on one call, you simply move on to the next one, simple. However, the difference between going through the mechanics of this task and achieving results can be huge.

I liken it to playing snooker. I can play snooker. I'm stood in front of a large table, and my job is to use the cue to hit that white ball against one of those coloured balls. Yes, of course I can do it. But there's a world of difference between being able to do it and being able to do it well. Let's just say that no snooker-happy amateur would ever have anything to fear from me! Therefore, being able to do something and being able to do it well are quite different things.

Prospecting, like many other things, is a process. It requires a set of skills in order to be able to do it effectively. Therefore, the more you understand the process and work it, and use your skills to be effective, the more successful you will be. It has many advantages compared with many other forms of marketing and building relationships with customers. But that still doesn't make it easy.

Over the years, I've been asked by many clients to help 'convert' their team from a largely inbound call-receiving operation to one which can be effective in making outbound calls. Typically, what will happen is that an organisation has a number of people already working on the phone. They might be from customer service or internal sales. The key thing is that they spend their working day dealing with inbound calls. Dealing with customers of course. The client may then find that business is getting quieter, and so they need to act. They have a telephone-based team in the office who they see as an underutilised resource.

The team will do their best to make themselves look busy, but the manager knows that they are just killing time. Plus of course the business needs more customers. So, the obvious thing to do is to get the team trained up to make some outbound calls. If I'm talking to a client on the phone and they describe this situation to me, the conversation will generally go like this

I will say, *"OK, I understand. And have you spoken to them about this proposed change?"*

The client will usually reply with a *"Yes."*

My next question is then, *"And how do they feel about that?"*

The usual response is, *"They don't want to do it."*

This is a clear indication that people may be happy to talk to customers on the phone all day every day, provided they are not initiating the call. They may be confident carrying out this activity and be incredibly good at it. But as soon as you change the dynamic and ask them to make outbound calls: in other words, to initiate the communication, the situation changes radically.

I've also had many members of telephone teams say to me that *"I wasn't employed to do this type of work."* They see it as being completely and utterly different. As different as if they were being asked to clean the toilets or work in the warehouse.

STORIES FROM THE FRONT

I have one client who conducted a reorganisation many years ago. This involved combining what was essentially a sales team with a customer service team. In order to give the company more flexibility and reduce the overall number of people they needed to employ, they decided to merge the two roles, and so everyone in the team now has to undertake elements of both sales and customer service. But even now, seven years later, the part of the team that were in customer service still complain vociferously about their sales role. It seems that they don't see selling as part of their job, and they don't want to be associated with it. Seven years! That's a lot of baggage to carry around.

Play the long game

It's important to view the sales process as a long game. In talking to your customers or prospects over the phone, you are aiming to build rapport and long-term working relationships. Of course, you want to get some orders along the way, and therefore it's important to maximise any opportunities that you uncover. Nevertheless, be happy with short or small iterative steps. Be satisfied that you are making progress with this new account. Don't expect every call to be a selling opportunity.

Be organised and prioritise the calls that you need to make. Live proposals should be your main priority. Make sure these are followed up in a timely way. The next priority will probably be to contact people who you have recently spoken to and sent out information. You have a reason for continuing the dialogue with this group. Ideally, you always want to add some new or colder calls to your mix of warm and follow-up calls. Just as you may plan out the plants in your garden for all-year-round colour, so you do similar when managing your own sales funnel.

The accepted wisdom is that you should have various prospects at different stages of the sales cycle. If you simply put all your effort into converting warm leads, you will soon find that you have nothing left. Some of your warm leads will convert into orders. Some of them won't. But then you run the risk of having nothing else to go at. So, consider how healthy your sales pot is.

Develop a clear plan

Follow a daily plan. Just sitting at your computer in the morning starting to consider who to phone will waste time, make you less productive, and demotivate you. Develop a system which allows you to prioritise your calls, using flags and filters. This doesn't need to be complicated. But, once you have fired up your computer, you should be good to go. Within a couple of minutes, you should be ready to make your first call. A good strike rate would be that an hour later, you have successfully made between 10 and 20 calls, and got through to two or three key people. And this is all from the comfort of your chair. What other form of marketing allows you to speak to two or three people in one hour who could potentially have a use for the types of products or services you sell?

Reassure yourself that B2B selling is quite different from the possibly seedier world of B2C. You are a professional, and you are attempting to speak to other professionals who, theoretically at least, could have a potential use for your products and services. This is so different from the world of B2C where you may be cold called at home by an untrained commission-only agent working to a script. They know nothing about you. They are simply working on the basis of attrition. Their employer takes the view that if they phone 1,000 people at random, some of them must have a potential use for their service. This is not the world you operate in.

In B2B it's about working to a long-term sales plan. It is about establishing credibility. You're building trust. As I have outlined earlier, high-pressure doesn't work in B2B sales, so, stay well away from it. Your aim is to strike up a conversation. Find out about them and their business. How they use the products and services that your organisation could provide. Listen, take notes, and have a chat. This will then give you the chance to inform them about what you can offer. If they're interested at this stage, you may well look to nudge the sales process forward a little. You might offer to send them some information via email or in the post. You could find out how serious they are about moving forward, by offering to go and see them. Or you might arrange to send one of your work colleagues in to meet them. Following that, a proposal may be prepared. You then follow that up and find out if they want to move ahead. If they do, great, you've now secured an order. If not, do your best to find out why, and then you simply start building the relationship for the next time. Don't give up.

I've covered the issue of notes back in Chapter 4, in the pre-call planning. I outlined the type of notes you need, and equally importantly, the type of notes you don't need. If you are well-organised and set high standards around the quality of your notes, it will pay dividends when you're making outbound phone calls. Remember my mantra about trying to make every call a warm call. Your ability to be able to do this depends entirely on the quality of your notes.

Dedicate sufficient time and effort to planning and conducting your prospect calls. If you just do half an hour twice a week and then leave it 10 days before making any other calls, you almost certainly won't make any progress. This is like going to networking and giving up after one meeting because nobody wants to buy anything from you. I recommend that prospect calls are made in batches of at least an hour at a time. Like any skill that you practice, it takes a while to get into the groove. I still find that if I have had a period of time away from the phone, such as being on holiday, my dial rate is usually lower when I first get back to phoning. My mind is still probably on holiday, and I find that I get more easily distracted.

The more sales activity you want to generate, the more marketing and prospecting you need to do. I have suggested elsewhere the benefit of recording the key statistics of all this activity. If you are part of a telephone team, or you employ a telemarketing or telesales team, you should have some form of KPIs in place already. If you work for yourself, it is of course entirely your choice.

Learn from others

Be prepared to learn from others as well. If you work within a team structure, you will frequently pick up tips and techniques by observing how your colleagues work. Especially if some of them achieve consistently higher results than you. Ask yourself, what is it they do that is different to what you do? In phoning, it is easy to make direct comparisons because you are all performing essentially the same job. If you work alone or you are self-employed, then chat to other people about how they get on with prospecting. Many other people are treading the same path as you, and therefore there is always much to learn by sharing experiences.

I'm often asked the question, how many people should a company employ to make outbound prospecting calls? This question is particularly relevant if your company is looking to set up this function for the first time. My advice is always to engage at least two people making outbound calls. Even if this means having two part-time people, rather than one full-time person. If you can have both of them in the office at one time for at least part of the week it will help them, and it will help you. Firstly, they gain the benefit of a shared experience. This is important if you want to develop the skills of both people. Secondly, it gives you, the manager, the chance to compare performances between the two personnel. If one person isn't achieving the results that you want, but they are the sole person performing this role, you can't really be sure of the cause. Yes, it could be them. It might be that they are just not right for the job. That's the easy thing to conclude. But there are many other factors that may impact their effectiveness. It might be that your data or targeting isn't good enough. It might be that the proposition they are putting to customers over the phone isn't very engaging. At least if you have two people, you will receive feedback from them about what they feel works. Plus, you can compare results. It is also easier to cope with holidays. If you only have one person undertaking this role, when they are away, then obviously all work stops.

Be prepared to refine your approach as well. You may find that certain things get customers more engaged than others. So, analyse what appears to work, and what doesn't. Keep your messages simple and concise. If you deal with customers face-to-face, you can study elements of body language, and of course you can demonstrate products to people. On the phone you don't have any of this. So, your verbal communication needs to be crystal clear. And, if you're making a significant number of calls regularly, you have every opportunity to refine this approach.

It is all a constant learning experience. I wish you well!

CHAPTER 11:

SELLING FOR CONSULTANTS

It may be that you are reading this book as somebody who provides some form of consultancy service. In this chapter I reflect on this as a service that has no physical form. You are probably selling something based on knowledge or intellect.

This provides some specific challenges. Most fundamentally, it means that you don't have a bright shiny product that you can display on your website and offer people. It probably also means that your fee structure is more opaque than many companies selling physical products, which may well be clearly priced on their website. It may also be your own business. The services you are promoting are ones that you will provide personally. You may be a solo operator, perhaps working from home trying to drum up business to keep the wolf from the door. I identify with this community strongly because I am part of it. This community has been good to me over the years.

So, this is, in some small measure, my attempt at offering some help back.

Many business consultants I meet have real difficulty making outbound telephone calls. This is compounded by working on your own, with no one to encourage you following a series of rejections on the phone. At least if you're in a room with a few other people carrying out the same function, the shared experience can make it more bearable.

The other defining characteristic about making phone calls to promote consultancy services is that you have a choice about whether to make prospecting calls or not. This can lead to indecision. If you're employed by a company in some form of sales office-based role, the bottom line is you need to make a certain number of calls every day. There will be certain KPIs around this, and the company will have set up systems to monitor and measure your progress. No excuses: it's your job and you simply have to get on with it. It's the same with many field-based sales roles. Sales teams often spend a set number of days each week making their own prospecting telephone calls. Again, there is no choice, and so it makes life more straightforward. In a well-run company there is support available, both physically and emotionally. None of this is the case if you're working for yourself.

Phoning if you are self-employed

What does telephoning represent for you if you are a self-employed business consultant? The first point is that you have choices around what marketing you do. You don't need to do any phoning at all if you don't want to! You could go networking. You could spend time and money on SEO for your website. You could go to industry exhibitions or write articles for trade magazines. You could spend money on trade advertising. You may already have sufficient work, perhaps even a large contract with somebody who you used to work for. You could spend your days working on improving your profile and your use of social networking sites such as LinkedIn. You might want to sponsor the local football or netball team. Especially if your child is a member of the team. These are just a few of the options open to you. They are literally endless.

My background is in marketing, and therefore I would always suggest that you look to do a healthy mix of most of these things. At least try each of them and find out if they work for you. You will learn a considerable amount from each marketing approach you try. Then ultimately your marketing mix must answer two important questions:

* How effective is this marketing for you?
* How much do you enjoy it?

There is a strong chance that these two aspects will be closely linked. If you're good at something, and it works for you, presumably you will enjoy it. And conversely, if you enjoy something, it probably means that you're in some form of natural groove. And this is probably because you are good at it, and it is effective.

Therefore, if the idea of making prospecting calls terrifies you, then don't do it! The beauty of being self-employed or freelance is that you can choose what work you take on and how you work. That's probably part of the reason you moved away from the employed world in the first place! You relish the freedom to be able to choose.

However, in my experience of working with many self-employed people, the reason it frightens you is that you've never had any training in order to help you be successful. So, this is a completely understandable human reaction. If you've been given no training in how to prepare, and you don't really understand the process or the structure of outbound prospecting calls, then it's entirely natural to feel hesitant about it.

The material I have given you in previous chapters is designed to help you understand the structure in more depth. And if this makes you feel more confident, then this will help.

Using the telephone to make prospecting calls to support your business *does* have many advantages. The obvious one is that you can carry out the work from the comfort of your home. It is very flexible. You can start when you want. You can finish when you want. It is also extremely cost effective. You already have a telephone, a computer and a broadband line. So, the fixed costs are already there. And the variable cost, that of making calls, these days is incredibly low. Probably cheaper than most other forms of marketing that you may consider. So, it has plenty going for it. You now need to make it effective. To make it work for you.

Have a plan

I've already acknowledged that you have no physical product to sell, so this makes conveying your marketing message more difficult. Do you simply say, *"I'm really good at this"*? Do you point out that you have 20 years of experience in your field of expertise? The answer to the second question is probably yes, but the first question is frankly, ineffective. Simply telling somebody over the phone that you are really good in a particular field is unlikely to persuade them. They will simply think, *"Well, you would say that wouldn't you?!"* You need to focus on specifics and talk facts.

Another defining feature of the business consultants I work with is that they are all intellectually bright. You would expect this if what they sell is a product of their intellect. Clearly then, struggling with phoning is not about intelligence. Most business consultants are also good communicators. So, it's also not about a lack of communication skills.

This therefore suggests that it's the process and structure of making the calls which is the issue. And the good news is that all of this can be learned and practised.

It's about having a plan and a good, robust structure in place. Many within the consultancy community talk about a fear of cold calling. That's perfectly understandable. So, why not start with warmer calls? Get some practice in with some people that you have met before. Chat to people who you have met through networking, or at a trade exhibition. Chances are, you will have many business cards that you have gathered over the years, plus all your contacts in LinkedIn of course. You don't need to start by calling total strangers. Phone some people who may even be pleased to hear from you! Even if they don't want to buy anything. It doesn't matter in the short term because all you're trying to do initially is start building relationships. As I've stated in earlier chapters, you need to establish rapport with them anyway, before they will feel comfortable in buying anything from you.

Planning is vital. The single most important thing you need to do is to compile a well-targeted list of people you want to contact. And each time you pick up the phone, you should have a clear idea of why you're calling them. Time spent defining and refining this list, in advance of picking up the phone, is a valuable investment. Build yourself some form of contact database. If calling is to become even a small part of your marketing activity, it makes sense to set yourself up properly. You may choose to invest in one of the many good CRM systems. Computers are perfect for logging your customer contact. However, if you're a SoHo (a solo operator operating from home), and only you use this information, then just using Excel may be more than adequate. As mentioned earlier, Excel has its limitations, particularly if you want to start filtering and targeting your marketing in detail. Whatever choice you make, the key thing is to get started!

Create your own call guide

A call guide is not so much a script that you're going to stick to rigidly, but more a checklist of the things you need to talk about. What are the things about you that will make people sit up and listen? Talk about the companies you've worked for in the past or have worked for as a consultant. Talk about your length and breadth of relevant experience and how well-established your business is. Talk about a well-known industry initiative that you have worked on. Come up with compelling reasons why people should engage with you at an early stage. Everything you say is designed to build your credibility relating to your field of expertise. You need to stand out from the crowd.

How to make very few cold calls

You may find it reassuring to know that I now make very few cold calls. However, I still spend a large amount of time on the phone, around 400 hours per year prospecting. How do I square these two facts? As soon as I start making calls and engaging in dialogue with people, I frequently need to call them back. Many calls result in some future action. They may say that they will talk to me again, but after their busy period. Or after they are back from their holiday. Or after the company merger with XYZ goes through. People are often interested in what I have to offer, but now just doesn't happen to be the right time. So, most of my calling is to people who I have called before. I guarantee that this will be your experience too.

Keep in touch with clients

Then of course there are all your current clients and all your previous clients to talk to. It's so important to keep in touch with all these people. It's an easy lead-in to ask them how they are and how business is at the moment. They will appreciate the fact that you're taking an interest and making time for them. And who knows what might happen? The fact that you're having a conversation with them may lead you to uncover another business opportunity. You have nothing to lose. So, in your contact database, the most important field ends up being the next call-back date. Then, each time you start a phoning session, you simply filter based on calls due today or on all previous days. This makes your working process so much more effective because it filters out any future calls due. You're now only looking at the people who you should be talking to. Incidentally, don't be too hung up on overdue call-back dates. If you don't have any specific projects on the go with somebody, and your next logged call-back date is the 12th, if you don't call them until the 20th or even the 25th, it really doesn't matter. Focus instead on those where you are following up a proposal or following up specific information that you've sent. Don't leave those too long. There are unlikely to be too many of these, and so it should be easy to keep track of them. And flagging them in your database should help too.

You will also need a field in your database to record your call notes. As I explained previously, these should be thorough but abbreviated. Don't write chapter and verse. You just need enough to refer to as you start your next call with them.

Building momentum

I have already recommended spending time on the phone in batches of at least an hour at a time. During this time, do not get distracted by other business activity. Don't check your emails, and don't allow yourself to get distracted and walk away from your desk. And your tea or coffee? Yes, on completion of your hour on the phone. The reason this is important is that you will find you build momentum to carry out this work. It's a form of mental exercise. Focusing in this way will help you to get into the rhythm of this type of work. Imagine if your trip to the gym was split up with many other activities. Going off to check your phone. Or hanging the washing out or feeding the dog. It just wouldn't deliver benefits in the same way. And so it is with phoning. You will find that mentally you start to get in the groove. You start to feel more comfortable with what you're doing, and how you're conducting your calls. While you're in this mental space, you're likely to do better if you keep going.

I also talked about, in Chapter 4, the need to keep a log of call activity. This is quite separate to what you enter in your CRM system. This is merely a tick-box exercise where you record your call and the result that you achieve. I do this every time I make outbound prospecting calls. One of the benefits of doing this is that it allows you to feel that you're making progress. Even if you have made 100 calls and spoken to perhaps 15 decision makers, you can at least see what you have achieved. For me personally it's motivating. It allows you to monitor your activity and relate your input to your outputs. Over a period of time, you can gauge how much time you need to spend on the phone and how many calls you need to make to achieve an acceptable commercial result. You need to know this ratio.

Be commercial

Another benefit of being a self-employed business consultant is that you probably don't need to have a set price list. This gives you immense flexibility. But it also gives you a potential headache. You will probably end up charging different companies different amounts for the same service. There is nothing wrong with this: it is what I refer to as 'opportunity pricing'. You may want to charge a larger corporate company a higher rate than a small local business. You might choose to help a small local company but know that they are not able to pay the type of fees you normally like to charge. So, what do you do? Do you walk away, on the basis that everyone should pay exactly the same? I suggest that you probably wouldn't. So, your fee structure needs to be agile.

You do need to work out what you need to earn over the course of a year to deliver the lifestyle that you want or perhaps need. Then set yourself some targets relating to the number of people that you need to work with. And then work out a level of phone call activity you need to make to help to achieve this goal. Your telemarketing, and indeed all other forms of marketing, should be an integral part of your plan to achieve your financial goals.

The fact that I record all my telemarketing activity, and have always done so, means that I can track a significant amount of useful data. At the end of each year, I can work out what value my phone activity has delivered, by dividing total revenue by the number of calls that I've made to produce that revenue. Using this data, you can also chart the lifetime value of your clients. All this helps to inform your decision-making.

Confirm in writing

As a business consultant, this is a golden rule for me: put everything commercial down in writing and send it to your clients and prospects. This is something that I have always done and, for the last 20 years or so, has served me well.

It's all-too easy, with elements of consultancy, for the agreement to be a little vague. Because there is no physical product, the boundaries between what you are undertaking to provide and what is outside that, can become blurred. In this grey area can be the difference between you making money on the project and not. Or worse, potentially tying yourself and your client up in legal knots.

As stated previously, I am a huge fan of templates. So, have your proposals and trading terms already set down in a document that you can simply copy and paste. This ensures you stay consistent, and that you don't miss anything. Keep one master document, and whenever you want to make changes always update the master document first. Years ago, not long after I'd started my business, I managed to land some customer service training work with a local council. They asked if I could send them details of my cancellation charges. *"Of course,"* I replied, *"I'll send them through."* As you can probably guess, I didn't have any at that point! So, I hastily wrote some and added them to one of my commercial templates. They were also added to the website.

The value of contracts?

When I've agreed some work over the phone, I always say to the customer that I will confirm the details in writing. That way, you eliminate the chances of misunderstanding. This protects you of course, but it's fairer for them as well. I've always shied away from having signed contracts with clients. My view is that if they change their mind and don't want to work with me anymore, then I don't want to make it complicated and go down the legal route. This goes against the advice of a member of my family, a legal eagle, but it's not caused me problems up to this point. I've only encountered two legal issues in 20 years of trading. In the first instance it wasn't even related to training. A business partner and I used to run a small, outsourced telemarketing agency. A client contested that we hadn't carried out the work agreed. So, he refused to pay. It went to court, and we won 80% of the fee, plus expenses. And in the second case, which was settled out of court with the client paying me most of the money, having a contract wouldn't have helped.

Always set down in writing what you will be providing, with a clear statement of the relevant fees, and any extras such as expenses where applicable. Once you've received an email back from your client agreeing to the work, then I suspect from a legal point of view you now have the agreement that you need. The benefit of being a consultant is that, because you don't have a physical product, you haven't generally incurred significant cost in order to deliver your service. What you stand to lose is only your time. If you are in any form of business where you need to make investment in equipment, or undertake a significant amount of pre-work, then ensure that an agreed contract is in place before commencing any work.

Keep in touch

Being a business consultant probably means that you have a relatively small number of clients at any one time, but with high value. This is quite different to the situation for a High Street retailer. They have many customers, who probably spend a small amount on each transaction. Building close personal relationships with such customers is difficult. For you it is much easier.

Use this to your advantage. Keep in touch on the phone periodically with your active trading clients and previous ones. Have a plan and a reason to call, and maintain this communication, even if it is periodic. And why wouldn't you? After all, keeping in touch on the phone is such an easy way to maintain contact. Look out for other opportunities too. If you specialise or niche in one specific industry sector, check out the various trade exhibitions that represent your sector. Phone some of the people that you have identified as target prospects to work with and agree to meet up with them for coffee at the exhibition. This is a way of staying on their radar and achieving a face-to-face meeting in a low-pressure neutral territory environment.

You might read articles in the trade press that relate to your clients or prospects. As has been suggested previously, send them details via email with an accompanying note, something along the lines of, *"I saw this and thought of you."* They will appreciate this. LinkedIn also prompts you with opportunities to keep in touch. Maybe somebody you haven't worked with for over a year has a work anniversary. You can congratulate them: nothing too gushy, but again it reminds them of your existence. Ensure you are connected with your current clients on LinkedIn. This gives you the opportunity to maintain contact in a light-touch way. However, be careful, as this does mean that you open up your client base to anyone who has access to your connections. If you're working to win a prospective client, you may want to leave connecting until after you've finished working with them. You don't want to risk opening up your sales pipeline to those who might want to steal clients from you. Something which can help here is to ensure that your connections are a broad mix of different people from different sectors of the business community. If you have over 1,000 connections, it should be quite difficult for a potential competitor to work out who the 10 or 12 are that you are actively working with.

Connect on LinkedIn

Cultivate a broad connection base on LinkedIn. Connect with people that you worked with when you were employed; with previous clients who have now moved on to other organisations; with friends and family who are also businesspeople; people who you socialise with or have met while networking. Build a pool of connections that is rich and wide. Keep your potential competitors out of this pool. Anyone who is a first-level connection has access to all your connections, so, be careful who you let in.

Make your contacts feel special

Anything you do which allows you to keep in touch without overtly selling will help you to maintain a relationship and rapport with your contacts. And, given that what you sell is you, it's important to work at this. Make them feel special. Nevertheless, this must be done in a natural way. If it comes across as being manipulative or solely for your own benefit, then it will be counterproductive.

How about getting them involved in your business when the opportunity comes along? You might be in the process of redesigning your website. Why not put it out to some of your present or previous clients, and ask for their views on it? After all, they are your target market. Ask for their advice on anything where you feel they may have valuable input. Your regular clients and ones who have treated you well in the past are the ones you should reward with special offers. For example, you might have an idea that you want to take to market. Perhaps you want to test it out on somebody first. An idea mentioned previously: why not offer it for free to a company which has looked after you in the past? There will be clients who appreciate what you do and support you. They always seem to be respectful, and they settle your invoices quickly. I am fortunate that I have many such clients. These are the ones you should reward by offering elements of added value. Although they are not necessarily going to become friends, it certainly does take the business relationship to a new level.

Be bold, be organised and spread the word. Your word!

CHAPTER 12:
SELLING IN A POST-PANDEMIC WORLD

This book has been written during the extraordinary year of 2020. Whenever it is that you are reading this book, it is likely that, even with the perspective of possibly a few years, business life can be looked upon as having been through a watershed moment during that year.

Predicting long-term trends and impacts in the world of business is notoriously difficult and so we have not let events of 2020 unduly influence the messages in this book. The central argument that "people buy from people" has not been shaken by world events. It is a fundamental human and business truth which underpins all the recommendations, tips and techniques relating to selling on the phone outlined in this book. However, there ARE some shifts which feel permanent, which will alter the way some of those tips and techniques are applied. We all need to think more creatively about our industry, our customers' needs and our business strategy.

The good news is that the telephone is likely to become a more significant business tool in a post-pandemic world. When we are allowed to mix freely, so much business is done face-to-face. That freedom disappeared during 2020. For example, I recall hearing an anecdote in October 2020, where a major corporate, Fujitsu, banned their staff from making any face-to-face contact. Or at least, they had to get written permission first.

As a result of all this, we have all started to become experts on the various meeting platforms such as Zoom and Microsoft Teams. Fortunately, and it's a credit to the developers of both of these software programmes, they are reasonably intuitive and easy to get to grips with. The use of these platforms is set to increase and is already part of the standard toolkit for organising meetings, selling and communicating with customers.

Organising on-screen conversations with people is the next best thing to physically being with them. However, it is not without its irritations. The technology can be problematic. It also takes longer to set up than a straightforward telephone call. If you are representing your company, you need to be conscious of the set-up and the background. The light, sound quality, and broadband speed all make a difference to the overall user experience. I recall one slightly unsettling experience with a new client during the initial UK lockdown, who had his camera placed on his desk at 90 degrees from where he had his screen. We were negotiating setting up a programme of training for his team online, and all I was able to see was the side of his head. Ultimately, I made the decision that this felt just plain weird and ensured that all future conversations were conducted on the telephone. So, these are some of the extra factors which we all need to think about.

A good friend of mine, who works for a large corporate bank, mentioned to me that he frequently paces up and down while he is having conversations with his customers on the phone. He finds this energising and believes that he is more creative while doing so. He is having to rethink his whole communication strategy when using Teams.

This is all still considerably quicker than travelling to see somebody, and a heck of a lot cheaper. Whether you are self-employed or employing a team of salespeople who traditionally operate out on the road, the savings on time and travel are extremely attractive. The whole nature and role of external sales teams are being completely re-evaluated as a result. For many companies, that fleet of company sales vehicles may soon be a thing of the past.

So where does this leave the role of the telephone call? If you are unable to visit your customers, the telephone is now the next best thing. So, seize this moment to use the telephone to maximum effect. At the time of writing I have already had conversations with clients who are concerned about how their sales teams are adapting and structuring their sales calls, when having to conduct these exclusively over the phone.

The hints, tips and techniques outlined in this book have therefore never been more relevant and more important. If reading body language and all those other advantages of a face-to-face meeting (and body language is remarkably hard to gauge on Zoom) are now inaccessible to the vast majority of businesses, then maximising the way you conduct a phone call is even more important than ever. Invest in developing telephone selling skills for you and your team NOW. It's never been a more important sales medium! Success on the phone will be determined by the amount of skill you deploy. The information in this book has shown that there is a considerable amount more to a good business call than simply phoning somebody up for a chat.

Change comes in many forms

So many aspects of people's working lives are changing. Consider the following:

- More people are working from home and will continue to do so
- Offices may be partially empty or closed, permanently
- Many customers have less money to spend

This provides you with challenges... and opportunities. Let us consider the impact of people working from home. You will frequently find that if the person you usually speak to is working from home, the receptionist or person who answers the call on the office number can't put you through. They're not being difficult. They simply can't. They may offer to take your details and say that they will *"email them on to Sarah/Phil/whoever."* Often the person taking the call is also working from home. You can frequently tell because of the background sounds or the acoustics. It often sounds very echoey.

Clearly, this limits your opportunities. I suggest that if you already have your contact's email address, you simply say that you will send an email. That way of course you control the content of the message. However, if you don't know the email address of the person you need to speak to, you will probably need to take their colleague up on their offer. Give them your contact details, and hope that this will get passed on.

All this means that you need to be more creative in how you reach them. Remember, these same difficulties are facing your competitors, and so if you can work around this more effectively than they can, you have created a clear business opportunity. The main two available methods of contact are their mobile or their email address. Mobile is preferable, of course, because it allows for a two-way conversation. Although I expressed reservations earlier in the book about calling people on their mobiles, if you're calling them during the working day, you should be OK. After all, we know they are working from home and so they will be geared up and ready to discuss work issues. You don't have to worry about calling them while they're in the middle of doing something else if they're working from home.

This is where it will have paid dividends to have harvested their mobile number and email address previously. Certainly, the rapid rise of the pandemic and the subsequent lockdown rewards anyone who has been diligent about noting these alternative methods of contact.

I have discussed with a colleague the difficulty of making contact with somebody on their mobile phone. He made the point to me that if he receives a call on his mobile and he doesn't recognise the number, he will often hesitate or avoid picking up the call. He asked me about this, on the basis that it's difficult getting hold of somebody on their mobile, as they will be selective about which calls they answer. This is certainly a challenge, but no more so than when you phone somebody in their office. You speak to the receptionist, and they probably filter the call by saying that your prospect is in a meeting or not taking sales calls. Or alternatively your prospective customer is sat in the office but leaves the call to go onto their answerphone. This forms an effective filter for them. So, trying to contact people on their mobile is no more difficult than calling them in the conventional office set-up.

Handle the situation in the same way as you would if they were in their office. Be prepared to play a long game and leave them messages. But don't call too frequently. As I've said in earlier chapters, if you've left a couple of messages and they've not come back to you, chances are they probably don't prioritise a conversation with you at this time. Nevertheless, you can always blend your communication with other forms of contact. So, you can drop them an email. Many people find it easier to respond via email than they do to call you on the phone. If they call you on the phone, you may answer, and this means they are forced into having a conversation with you. Particularly when they have nothing much to say to you, they will probably try to avoid this.

It is now no longer true that companies cannot operate without staff in the office. Even for companies which supply products, they have opted to keep their offices shut, even though the warehouse or production facility was back up and running again. As with all human activity, new ways of adapting and changing behaviour and systems have arisen, with remarkable speed and ingenuity.

Handling a recession

Many people don't have a lot of money to spend, post-pandemic. Post-pandemic, any recovery in buyer activity in many B2B sectors is likely to be slow and painful. The irony is of course, that a recession is defined as 2 consecutive quarters of negative growth. However as an economy tries to get back on its feet post-pandemic, there will be some growth of course. However it's from such a low base, that although the situation is better, it is still dire. So, while there might not be talk in the media of a recession, buyer activity will still be low.

The highs and lows of economic growth and shrinkage have been of an unprecedented nature during 2020 and probably beyond. Where measurements of growth or recession in a mature Western economy such as the UK has usually been measured in single digit percentage point shifts, we have now witnessed double-digit shifts. With so much seismic disruption to so many business sectors, on a scale not witnessed previously in our lifetimes, we all need to tear up the rulebook and think creatively. Think carefully about the sectors in which you operate. Chances are that many will be in a desperate situation. The aviation, tourism and hospitality industries have been devastated by the effects of Covid-19. Conversely, there are sectors which are not only surviving, but thriving, DIY, banking and takeaway food businesses for example.

Spend some time working out the current winners and losers among your customer and prospect base. Work out what they do and how they are now operating and adapting. If you have a good relationship with these customers, you will know this sort of information off the top of your head.

It doesn't need to be a forensic analysis. What this will do, though, is save you wasting considerable time pushing against locked doors. On the positive side, it will help you to identify and prioritise new opportunities emerging in those sectors which are in growth, or are even new services being offered in this new post-pandemic world. In the past you may have had to wait for decisions and orders. However, in the 'new normal' things may have speeded up in months, weeks or even days! Such circumstances favour the brave, the innovative, the alert and the adaptive among us, all traits I have been promoting anyway throughout this book.

So, those clients or prospects which are suffering severely, you need to leave dormant, particularly if you sell some form of added-value product or service. You can push as hard as you want, and be as skilful as you can, but if they simply do not have the money right now your efforts will be wasted. I still suggest that you keep in touch with these customers from time to time though. You don't even need to mention your products or services. Your intention is to simply show concern and reassure them that you are thinking about them. With any form of selling it's always important to remember, as we highlighted at the beginning of this chapter, that **people buy from people**. So, be human and take an interest. They will appreciate this. Just as people lying in a hospital bed like receiving visitors, so your customers who are in desperate straits will also be perhaps both surprised and pleased that you've bothered to keep in touch. They know that you know you're unlikely to gain any revenue from them at this stage. Then, when the economic sunshine comes out again after the metaphorical rain, your relationship with them will likely be stronger in the future. I also think that just staying in touch with people can frequently lead to other conversations that you could never predict. So, do the right thing and be a nice person. See Chapter 3! Ultimately it will work in your favour.

Market segmentation needs to be thought out much more carefully than it did before. If you tend to specialise in a sector that has been severely affected by the pandemic, you need to be more creative with how you package your solutions. The first thing is to review your pricing. This doesn't mean getting your prices as low as they can possibly be. Trying to save somebody else's business at the risk of making yours insolvent is not a great strategy.

But you could offer your product or service in bite-sized chunks, or smaller batches, to make it more affordable. Offering just-in-time delivery so that your customers don't have to carry large stock perhaps. How about offering them payment terms where they pay a set amount each month? It's difficult to go into much more detail than this, because it depends on what product or service you offer.

Find out what other companies are doing. Not necessarily your competitors but check out how friends' businesses are dealing with the same challenges in other industries. Other people will come up with great solutions, some of which may work for you. You may end up offering solutions or product offerings which you have never done before. This indicates that you are adjusting to this very different world. You may well have heard the phrase that *"the definition of madness is to keep doing the same thing and expect a different result."*

So, fortune favours the brave, now more than ever before. With your colleagues, reassess every element of your business process and your product or service offering.

- What does the market want now?
- Where is the market heading?
- What specialisms do you and your company offer that you can trade on?

Be bold and embrace change

During the Covid-19 pandemic the phrase 'pivoting the business' was used frequently, which I'd not heard before. You may need to take your business in a completely different direction, based around some of your existing in-house expertise. We have all seen the examples, during the pandemic, of engineering companies turning their hand to making components for ventilators or other products desperately needed by the NHS. Even British Formula One engineering companies grabbed the headlines for helping out with their expertise.

This huge economic change is a shifting of the tectonic plates of business. I liken it to stirring the pot. In this turmoil, it is the innovators and entrepreneurs who will spot opportunities and float to the top. They will work out where the market is heading and start orientating their business accordingly. Whilst we won't all necessarily be the next George Soros, Richard Branson, or Elon Musk, we can still take actions to ensure that we stay ahead of the game. And in fact, just keeping our heads above water as a business until things improve will constitute a great achievement.

The very best of luck.

Printed in Great Britain
by Amazon